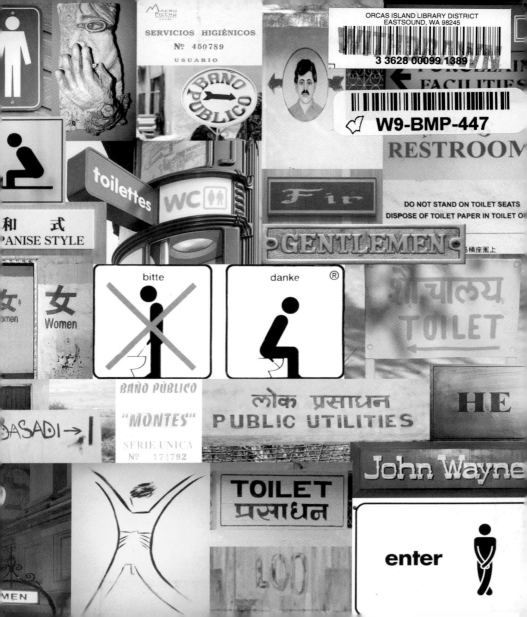

Toilets of the World

Swirling, swirling, around and around and around and down

Morna E. Gregory and Sian James

Toilets of the World

MERRELL

LONDON · NEW YORK

First published in 2006 by
Merrell Publishers Limited

Head office
81 Southwark Street
London SE1 0HX

New York office
49 West 24th Street, 8th Floor
New York, NY 10010

merrellpublishers.com

Publisher Hugh Merrell
Editorial Director Julian Honer
US Director Joan Brookbank
Sales and Marketing Manager
  Kim Cope
*Associate Manager, US Sales
  and Marketing* Elizabeth Choi
Art Director Nicola Bailey
Designer Paul Shinn
Managing Editor Anthea Snow
Project Editors Claire Chandler,
  Rosanna Fairhead
Editor Helen Miles
Production Manager
  Michelle Draycott
Production Controller
  Sadie Butler

All illustrations copyright © 2006
Sian James, with the exception
of the following:
Page 8: Galleria Borghese,
Rome, Italy/Lauros/Giraudon/
The Bridgeman Art Library;
page 9: Fotomas Index;
page 11: © thomas-crapper.com;
page 12: Lucinda Lambton/
arcaid.co.uk;
page 13: Courtesy of Twyford
Bathrooms

British Library Cataloguing-in-
Publication Data:
Gregory, Morna, E.
Toilets of the world
1.Outhouses 2.Toilets 3.Public
comfort stations
I.Title II.James, Sian
696.1'82

ISBN-13 978-1-8589-4337-4

ISBN-10 1-8589-4337-X

Designed by James Alexander
at Jade Design

Copy-edited by
Kirsty Seymour-Ure

Printed and bound in China

Jacket back, clockwise from top:
*Dune 45, Sossusvlei, Namib
Naukluft Park, Namibia* (see
pages 134–35); *Nalunega Island,
San Blas Archipelago, Panama*
(see page 85); *Singel Canal and
Brouwersgracht, Centrum,
Amsterdam, The Netherlands*
(see pages 128–29); *Terratima
Lodge, Rocky Mountain House,
Alberta, Canada* (see pages 48–49)
Page 2: *Detail of Merrill Mason's
public washroom entitled*
Emptying and Filling, *John
Michael Kohler Arts Center,
608 New York Avenue,
Sheboygan, Wisconsin, USA*
(see also pages 30–31)

Contents

**Loo, john, dunny, privy, bathroom, lavatory, outhouse, WC,
longdrop, commodities, powder-room, crapper, throne,
porcelain god, washroom, toilet, can, urinal, facilities, pisser,
comfort station, head, water-closet, little boys' room, shitter,
pot, nettie, bog ...**

So many names refer to the same mundane object. This
boundless terminology reflects human beings' natural
fascination with the toilet. Taboo subjects that have provoked
deep interest throughout the ages are known by many
names – consider death, drugs and copulation, to name a few.
Terms for the toilet all describe the smallest room in the house,
in the backyard, on the boat, or elsewhere. This list is from
English alone. To compile a complete list of toilet terminology
from all languages would fill volumes. Regardless of how it is
referred to, the universal aspect cannot be denied: every
human being on earth uses the toilet.

Why toilets? The subject is not nearly as frivolous as it may
appear at first glance. Toilets are bay windows with a view
on to a given population. The term 'toiletology' has yet to be
coined, although the study of toilets provides a cultural and
sociological analysis of the people who occupy different
regions throughout the world. The variety of toilets in different
countries is astounding. Toilets often (though not always)
reflect the development of a given country or region via design,
placement, material and mechanics. Aren't toilets the same
everywhere? In a limited geographical area, perhaps. On an
international scale, toilets are very, very different.

The use of the toilet transcends all race, religion, age and
social class. From the most impoverished to the highest
royalty, each and every one of us bows to the basics of bodily
function. Whether one does so in a ditch or on a jewel-
encrusted throne, the result is the same. The president, the
cashier, the supermodel, the writer, the lawyer and the farmer
all find themselves subject to this most basic of acts. It is

physical gratification from the earliest age on up. The act is philosophical – emptying the body empties the head as well. For how many busy and stressed people is this moment one of the few instants of solitary relief, privacy and contemplation in an otherwise hectic day? Many people confess to having great thoughts, ideas and insights while seated on the toilet.

Why do pigs clean toilets in India? Why are there entire fields of toilets in South Africa? Why are there toilets made of solid gold in Hong Kong? Why are there so many toilets on stilts in Panama? Why don't the Turkish use toilet paper? Why do the French squat? Why do the Costa Ricans squat? Why don't Brazilians flush toilet paper? Why do Japanese toilets have eight buttons? Why do urinals pop up out of the ground in London? Why does the space shuttle make 'people patties'? The answers to these probing questions lie within. Through the pages that follow, take a fascinating and explicit voyage through societies around the globe, continent by continent. A deeper cultural understanding of the world is within reach via the most raw and honest tattle-tale of human civilization: the toilet.

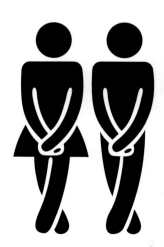

A history of toilet habits logically begins with the day the ancestors of the human race got up and walked away on two legs. These prehistoric beings probably gave little thought to where they would go to the toilet. Surviving evidence of the toilet habits of the earliest humans is scarce, but it is assumed that they just darted off to the most convenient bush, field or river. Only when people started living together in sizeable sedentary communities would the issue of 'where to go' have arisen. Not for health reasons — knowledge of bacteria and disease was aeons away — but because of the smell. Fortunately, humans have a natural aversion to their own waste, thus somewhat limiting the spread of disease. From the earliest civilizations, people have had to deal with the problem of waste disposal.

It is worth noting that this history of the toilet largely describes the evolution of the flush toilet — a luxury inaccessible even today to the majority of people on earth. The oldest known flush toilet is that of the palace of Knossos on the island of Crete, home of King Minos. The palace, dating back to 1700 BC, had four drainage systems, which emptied into great stone sewers. Its extravagant bathrooms enjoyed hot and cold running water, and fountains made with gold, silver and exquisite jewels. The palace toilet had a wooden seat and a water reservoir. Unfortunately, this technology was lost or ignored, and it took thousands of years for the flush toilet to resurface.

The earliest recorded guidelines on the disposal of human waste are attributed to Moses. As recorded in the Old Testament, he suggests to his people: "Thou shalt have a

Although it didn't make the cut for his Ten Commandments, Moses did advise his people to use the toilet away from the campsite and to bury that which came forth.

place also without the camp, whither thou shalt go forth abroad. And thou shalt have a paddle upon thy weapon; and it shall be when thou shalt ease thyself abroad, thou shalt dig therewith, and shall turn back and cover that which cometh from thee." (Deuteronomy 23: 12–13) Evidently the importance of doing one's business away from living quarters was already an issue in 1500 BC.

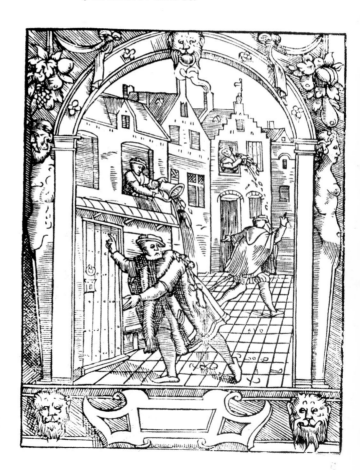

Courteous men walked on the kerb side to protect women from the contents of chamber pots hurled from windows above.

Five hundred years later, waste disposal in cities was a problem that could not be ignored. Jerusalem had an established network of drains and pipes to carry sewage from homes. These were emptied regularly and the contents carted through the 'dung gate' of the city, where a monumental heap accumulated.

The ancient Romans are renowned for their impressive feats of engineering. Rome's first sewer, the Cloaca Maxima, was built around 800 BC and still flows under the streets of Rome today. There is evidence of complex water management systems throughout the former Roman Empire, including latrines with running water. With the fall of the empire towards the sixth century AD, the golden days of baths and sanitation also crumbled. The lands were overrun by barbarians, and basic hygiene plunged into a long and dark decline.

The Middle Ages, from about AD 500 to about 1500, were vile and reeking in their lack of sanitation. In rural areas, people squatted outside some distance from their dwellings. Eventually they turned to using privies built over pits, a practice that still survives in some places today. Communal latrines were frequently found in areas where families lacked the means for their own private privy. Little thought was given to waste disposal, which became increasingly problematic in cities as populations grew. Disease was common. The terrible epidemic of bubonic plague of the mid-fourteenth century, later known as the Black Death, wiped out a large part of the population of Europe within a few years as a result of unsanitary living conditions. It was a time of festering open sewers, great dung piles and rivers so gorged with waste that they stagnated.

Chamber pots were in standard use, and the contents were usually heaved out of the window with a warning cry of "gardy loo!" – a term borrowed from the French *gardez l'eau*, meaning 'watch the water'. The word 'loo' has remained the staple slang for toilet in Britain. The wealthy living in castles had 'garderobes', latrines protruding from high up on the castle wall. The waste fell into the moat far below, helping to deter invaders from swimming across. Towards the end of this era, close stools were all the rage among the affluent: often sumptuously decorated and fitted with seats of velvet, essentially these were removable chamber pots built into a box with a lid. This enabled the user to sit rather than squat while using the facilities.

As the Middle Ages drew to a close, the scientific community made the connection between disease and poor sanitation. Laws were passed prohibiting open cesspits and the practice of throwing waste into the streets. However, the laws were hardly enforced and these abhorrent practices persisted for quite some time. Certain regions made one privy per house mandatory, with each dwelling to have a proper cesspit. The contents of the pits were collected and later used as fertilizer. Efforts to reform sanitation standards ultimately resulted in improved facilities, notably the reinvention of the flush toilet.

In England in 1596, Sir John Harington designed and built a flush toilet with a water reservoir. He was the favoured godson of Queen Elizabeth I and he installed his invention for her in Richmond Palace. She allegedly quite enjoyed the practicality of the device but, incredibly, Harington was ridiculed for his 'offensive' invention and never made another one. It took nearly 200 years for a similar device to be resurrected.

A history of the toilet, however brief, would be incomplete without a reference to the iconic Thomas Crapper. He was an accomplished inventor of sanitary wares, but he did not invent the toilet, as popular belief suggests. Although a debated theory, it is possible that Mr Crapper's name is the origin of the words 'crap' and 'crapper'. American soldiers stationed in Britain during World War I supposedly grew used to seeing

Although he did not invent the toilet, Thomas Crapper did perfect the water-saving valveless 'Water Waste Preventer'.

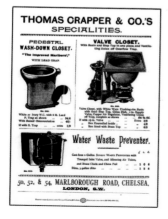

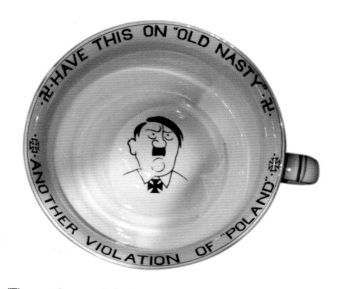

A certain satisfaction was gained from using a chamber pot bearing the image of a sworn enemy.

"Thomas Crapper & Co." emblazoned on porcelain toilets and before long they were excusing themselves to go to the Crapper. Thomas Crapper & Co. thrives today, specializing in exact replicas of sumptuous Victorian loos.

Toilet habits changed little after Harington's ill-fated invention and people continued to use privies, close stools and chamber pots. It was not until 1775 that the flush toilet reappeared, patented again in England by Alexander Cummings. Society was finally ready to embrace this avant-garde invention. Early water-closets (WCs) had their share of growing pains, but they were constantly being improved. Although the Victorians were faced with serious sewage disposal problems, this was an era when ornately decorated toilet bowls flourished as status symbols.

From Britain the flush toilet spread, albeit slowly, to the colonial countries, and was eventually adopted with varying degrees of prevalence elsewhere in the world. There have been no great changes since the late nineteenth century, except in bowl design, cistern shapes and the quantity of water used. The market now offers shredder toilets, compactor toilets, toilets made of gold, self-cleaning toilets, toilets with heated seats and toilets with built-in spray jets and blow-dryers. Such attention to detail is hardly strange for an object on which a person spends on average three years of his or her life.

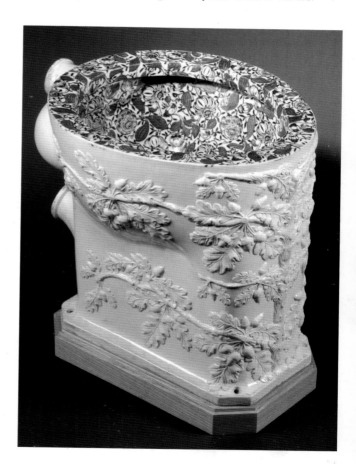

Victorian porcelain manufacturers made the toilet into a stunning work of art.

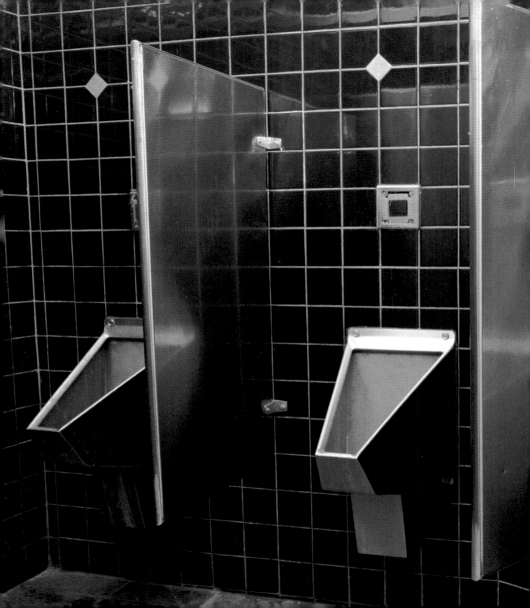

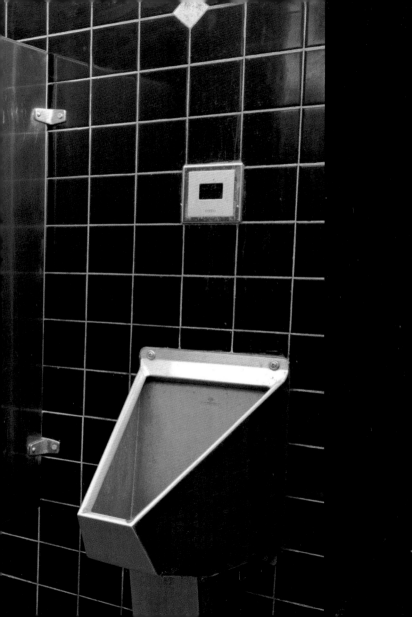

Things in North America are larger than life. Highways, houses, landscapes, vehicles, people, parking lots, refrigerators, shopping malls and ideas are all grandiose on this vast and wealthy continent. The volume of water that remains in the bowls of North American toilets is also extravagant. Visitors from other continents often comment on the unpleasant splash-back effect caused by this high water level. The amount of fresh water used for flushing the toilet is the largest in the world. The USA alone flushes eighteen billion litres of potable water every day. Until 1980, North American flush toilets used a whopping 19–26 litres (5–7 gallons) of water per flush, but government regulations have gradually diminished this volume to its present 6 litres (1.6 gallons) per flush as of 1994. While this is admittedly an improvement, North Americans still lead the world in excessive water consumption.

Conservation of fresh water was hardly a concern when North America was a land of outhouses. Most homes had a privy in the backyard and many continued to use this well into the mid-twentieth century. With the abundance of timber throughout the land, it was most often made of wood. All North Americans are familiar with the crescent moon cut out of the top of the outhouse door. In the days before electricity, an opening of some sort was necessary to let in light. Although the origins of the symbol are European and the moon is still found on some Old World outhouses, it is closely associated with the North American privy. The crescent moon is thought to have stemmed from the ancient pagan symbol for womanhood. A sun or a starburst was used for men's outhouses, but the men's fell more quickly into disrepair and both sexes tended to end up using the women's. The gender meaning was gradually lost and by the end of the nineteenth century, the moon was the symbol systematically carved into outhouse doors. Almost without exception houses are now plumbed, yet the outhouse remains a nostalgic feature of the rural landscape. Brand new, modern outhouses are found throughout the many national parks and wilderness retreats in North America.

Unlike the rest of the world, North Americans generally avoid using the word 'toilet' whenever possible. Often causing confusion outside America, they refer to the toilet as the bathroom, washroom, restroom, and even in Mexico, the *baño* (bath). Overseas, when a North American asks for the bathroom in an establishment, the host or waiter is baffled as to why the patron should want to take a bath. This terminology is probably related to the North American convention of installing toilets in the same room as the bath or shower, as opposed to many other regions in the world, where the toilet occupies its own little room. The reason for this is a mystery, but it is certainly not owing to a lack of available space. Despite the relative expanse in which North Americans live, their choice of toilet siting could be related to their love of proximity – the less far one has to go, the better. Another oddity of North American toilets is that although the majority of people are right-handed, the flush handle is always on the left.

The innovative North Americans are constantly creating ever more surprising toilets. Decorating trends to create unique venues of a particular ambience have led to toilets with television screens in the floor, urinals for women, toilets painted by artists, two-storey toilets, and water-wheel urinals. Modes of transportation also contribute to the palette, with the toilets of the international space station, submarines, and aircraft carriers. Each of these toilets fits a specific niche in place or time and offers a deeper perspective of the North American cultural psyche from an angle few would think to consider.

CBGB
315 Bowery Street
Lower East Side
Manhattan
New York City
New York

Stickers from every punk and underground rock band that ever played this venue plaster the walls, tables and washrooms of this legendary bar. The toilet is mounted like a throne on a raised brick pedestal in the massive private stall. CBGB was the haunt of the 1970s New York punk scene and gradually made the transition to rock. It was, and still is, a haven of artistic freedom and expression, launching such legends as Blondie and the Ramones.

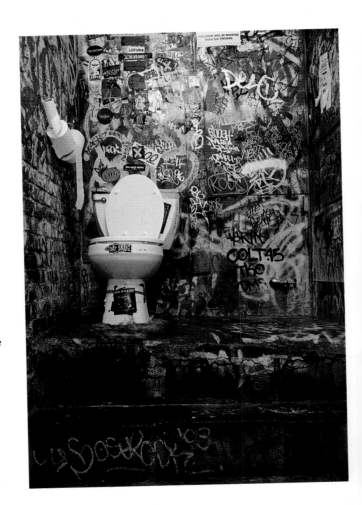

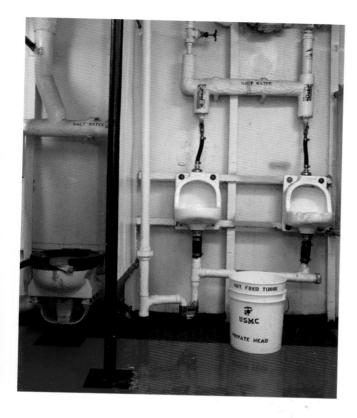

**USS _Hornet_ aircraft carrier
Pier 3, Alameda Point
US Naval Air Station
Alameda
California**

In seafaring jargon, toilets on board ships are known as 'heads'. During her time at sea, the _Hornet_'s toilet flushing mechanisms used salt water and evacuated everything out to sea. These heads were the domain of the Marine Corps aboard this WWII aircraft carrier. As shown by the bucket on the floor, Sergeant Tonge was deemed high-ranking enough to warrant his own pot to piss in.

The _Hornet_ was feared by the enemy as the "grey ghost", and during the war her aircraft shot down 1410 Japanese planes. On a more peaceful note, she plucked the astronauts of Apollo 11 from the sea after they had become the first men to walk on the moon.

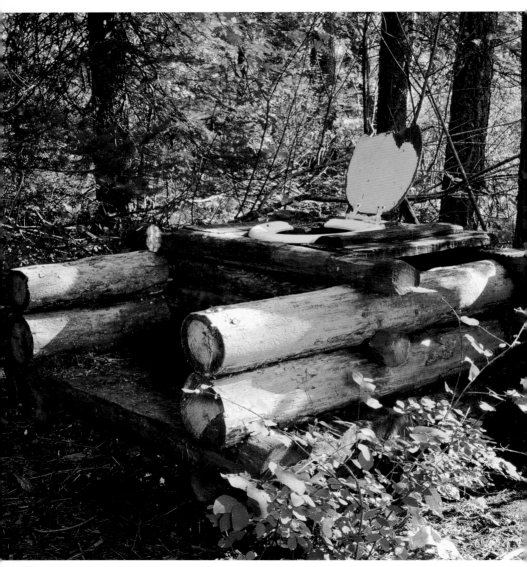

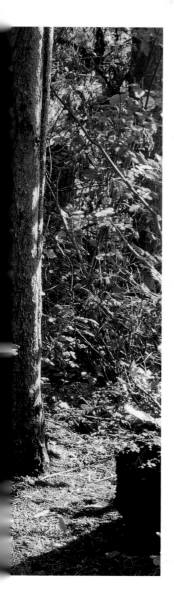

Service Road
White Ram Forest
Premier Lake Provincial Park
Purcell Mountains
British Columbia

With foliage providing the
only cover, users of this bush
toilet need to make as much
noise as possible to warn
anyone in the vicinity
(including bears) that it's
occupied. The rustic log
pedestal is the public toilet
of the nearby mountain hot
springs. Not a single nail was
used in its erection. The
massive logs stack tightly
together with saddle notches,
the same method used in
building log homes. Thanks
to such robust construction,
the toilet easily withstands
year after year of freeze
and thaw.

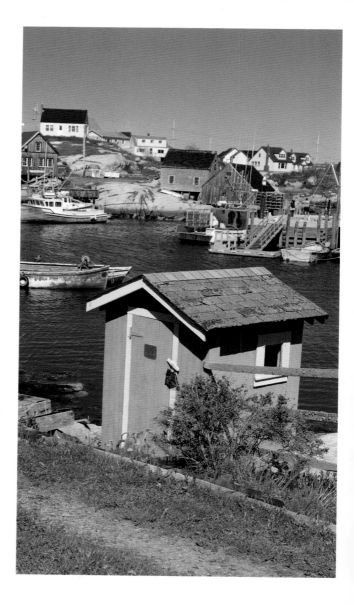

**Peggy's Cove
South Shore
Nova Scotia**

Authentic fishing villages
such as Peggy's Cove, with its
population of just 120 hardy
souls, dot the rugged Atlantic
coastline. Visitors from
around the globe are drawn
here by the tranquil beauty
and idyllic maritime scenery.
Most of the houses in Peggy's
Cove still have an outhouse in
the backyard. This one is
perched on the edge of the
rocks overlooking the cove. It
is protected from the ravages
of the seasons and the sea by
its sheltered location on a
narrow ocean inlet.

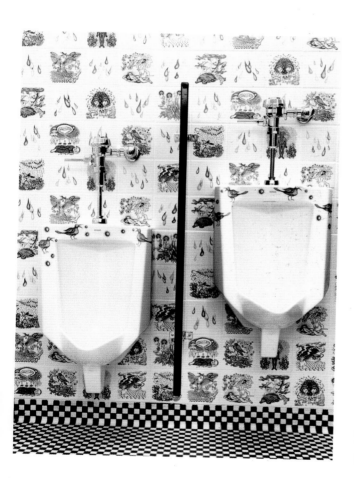

**Smith College
Museum of Art
Elm Street
Northampton
Massachusetts**

Designed by local artist Sandy
Skoglund, this striking black
and white public men's room
tells creation stories from
across cultures. Ten different
tile motifs portray historical
and geographical variations
on beliefs in humankind's
origins: Arctic, African,
Australian, Scandinavian,
Indian, Mayan, Egyptian,
Native American, Greek and
Chinese legends of the dawn
of humanity are all told via
the medium of these lively
pictorial bathroom tiles.

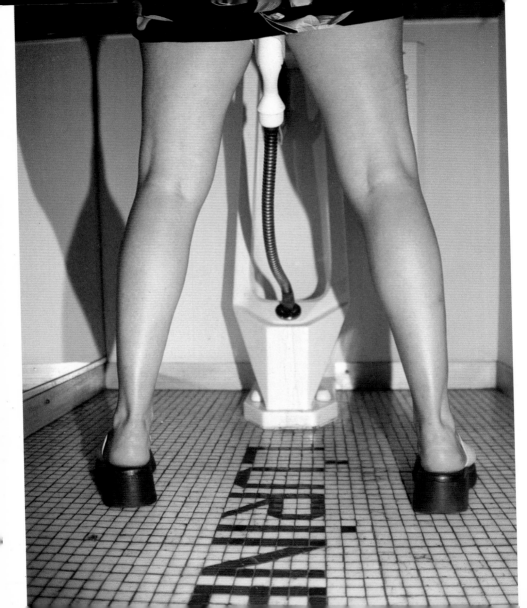

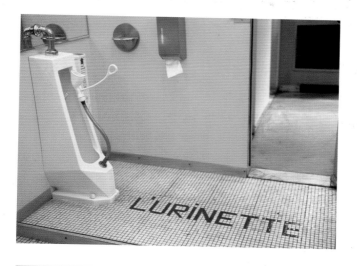

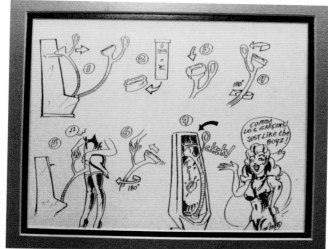

Above: L'urinette, *the urinal for women.*

Below: Directions for use.

Whiskey Café
5800 Blvd St Laurent
Montréal
Québec

L'urinette is one of the rare models of urinal designed for women. After the initial shock of this scary contraption, it proves to be as simple as the diagram on the wall. Pull down the handle, ladies, and turn it towards you. Take a paper cover from the dispenser and fit it over the cup. Use the handle to hold it in place and go. To finish, turn the handle back and release. The paper cover comes off, the handle snaps back into place and all flushes away automatically. "Just like the boyz!"

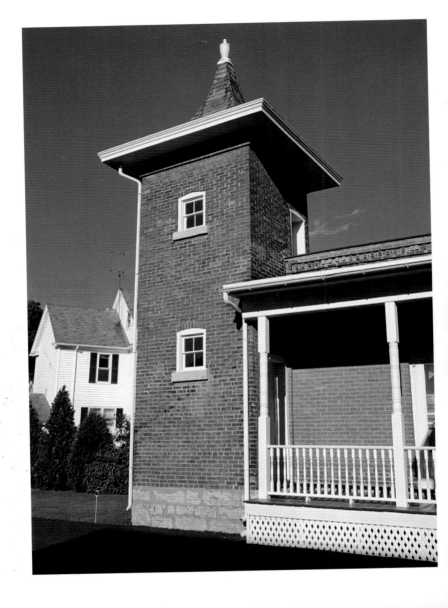

66 Main Street
Phelps
New York

This two-storey brick column is the outhouse attached to the back of a late nineteenth-century upstate New York home. Each level has three toilets and the top floor is accessible from the upstairs bedrooms by a walkway. Those using the bottom level needn't have feared – contents from above dropped through pipes in the wall to an underground pit. Perhaps such a spacious facility was a necessity in a town that considers itself the sauerkraut capital of the world.

Both levels of this two-storey outhouse have three seats.

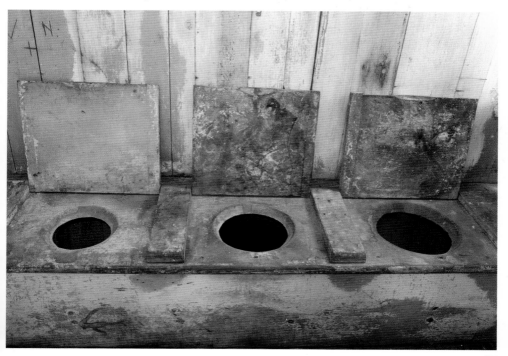

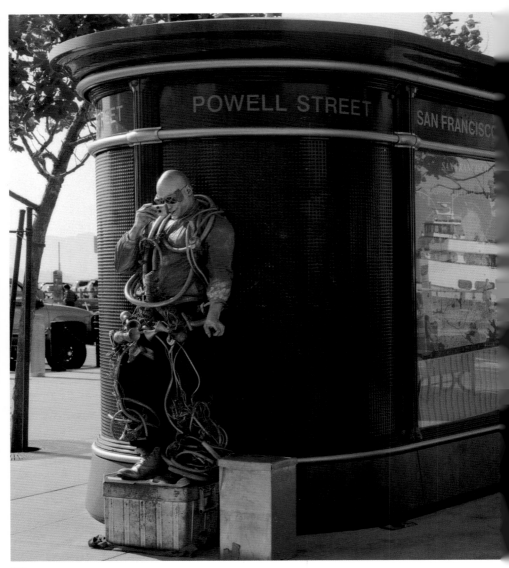

**The Embarcadero
Fisherman's Wharf
San Francisco
California**

For fifty cents, the visitor
can escape the crowds of
San Francisco's Fisherman's
Wharf by hiding out in this
automated public toilet. For
fifty cents more, the street
performer disguised as a
statue comes to life, bursting
into robotic clicks, whistles
and jerks. On the horizon,
the forbidding prison of
Alcatraz can be seen across
San Francisco Bay.

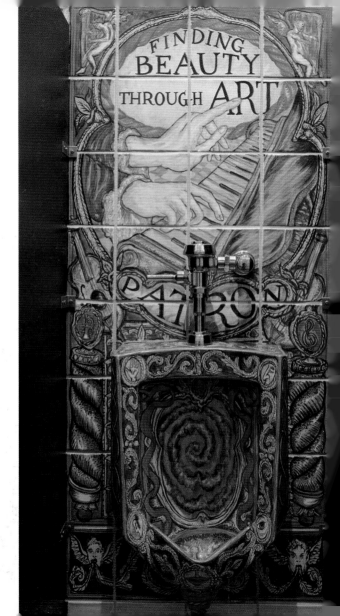

**John Michael Kohler
Arts Center
608 New York Avenue
Sheboygan
Wisconsin**

All six of the public washrooms in this arts centre are works of art themselves, each by a different artist and with its own theme.

This entire restroom is a work of art by New York artist Matt Nolen, entitled *The Social History of Architecture*. The urinal is covered, from floor to ceiling to fixtures, in a vibrant fresco. The paintings follow the evolution of architectural styles through the ages, from ancient Egypt to the present. Leaders from different periods are symbolically portrayed, so the user can imagine himself as a pharaoh, pontiff or corporate executive.

30

Brooklyn artist Ann Agee reflects upon the era of Delft ceramics with her creative blue-on-white tiled washroom. Her motifs depict the various roles that water plays in Sheboygan, whose residents live on the shores of Lake Michigan. Walls, washbasins, toilets and urinals all portray the theme of water with wit and humour. Bottled water, sprinkler systems and squirt guns are styled into an intriguing blend of techniques from the past and objects of the present.

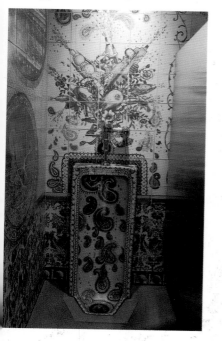

Urinal from Ann Agee's Sheboygan Men's Room.

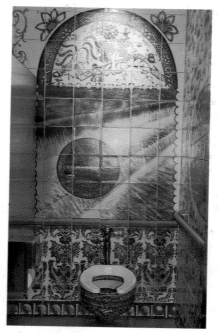

Toilet from Ann Agee's Sheboygan Men's Room.

Dutch Hollow Road
Rustic Road 56
Kickapoo Valley
Vernon County
Wisconsin

A toilet from a region called Kickapoo is a must. Built by the Amish, this brand new, well-made wooden outhouse is for sale for $350. Typical of North American outhouses, it features the crescent moon carved into the door. First migrating to North America from Europe in the early 1700s, the Amish settled in this particular area around 1920. The people of this quiet and reserved religious sect live off the land and sell home-made goods such as this outhouse. They reject electricity and other modern amenities, travel by horse and buggy, and, with increasing difficulty, insulate themselves from the outside world.

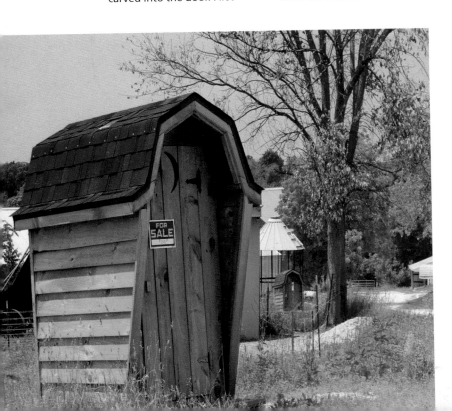

L'Avenue
922 rue Mont-Royal Est
Montréal
Québec

After an agonizingly long wait to use this restroom, the reason for the eternal delay became clear: the previous occupant was absorbed in a television programme. While seated, users can watch re-runs of *The Dukes of Hazzard* on a television screen built into the floor at their feet. The toilet seat is the standard split-front variety found in most public toilets throughout North America. The split seat is supposedly more hygienic as it collects fewer wayward drops for the user accidentally to sit on.

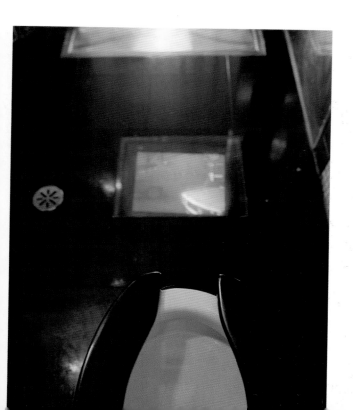

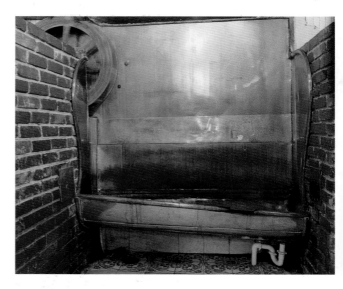

Madonna Inn
100 Madonna Road
San Luis Obispo
California

The kitschiest, tackiest hotel in the county is charming in its eccentric, over-the-top, all-American fashion. Visitors from the world over stop by this inn that screams with abrasively clashing colour, just to get a glimpse of the toilets. This unique crooked copper urinal is equipped with a perpetually spinning water wheel: water flows over the top of the wheel and down the wall, constantly flushing out the trough.

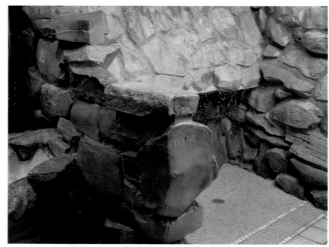

Men revert back to the Stone Age while using this Flintstones-like rock waterfall.

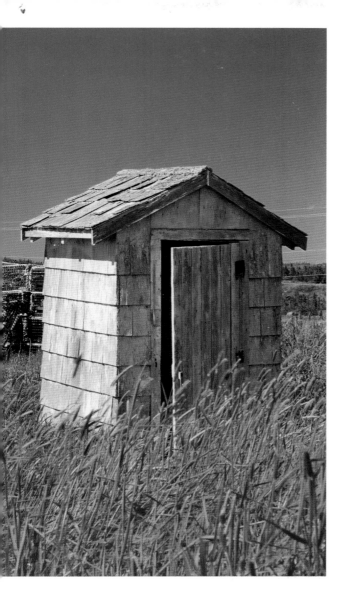

**Peggy's Cove
South Shore
Nova Scotia**

Lumber is an abundant
natural resource in North
America, so outhouses are
nearly always made of wood.
This weathered old toilet has
withstood the gales of the
maritime climate for decades.
Behind it are stacks of lobster
traps. Life in Nova Scotia is
tied in closely with the
Atlantic Ocean, and lobster
fishing is a major local
industry.

35

Bar 89
89 Mercer Street
SoHo
New York City
New York

The toilets of this swanky cocktail bar will strike fear into the hearts of the bashful. When the stall is vacant the doors are transparent, implying that everyone will have a clear view into the stall. Only when the latch is turned to lock do they suddenly become opaque. Confronting another fear of the bashful, this washroom does not segregate men from women. Half the stalls are pink and the other half are blue; inside they're all the same, despite their different hues.

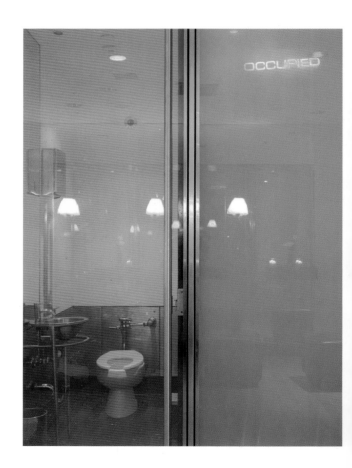

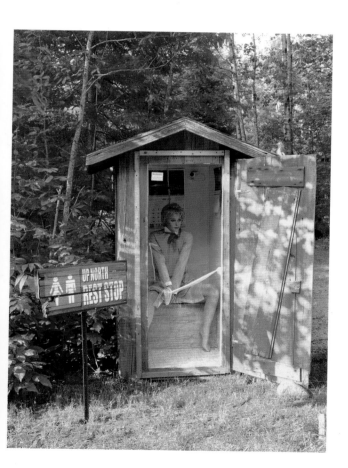

Keith Siding Road
Crandon
Wisconsin

The wait for the "Up North Rest Stop" is a long one indeed as the lady within is in no hurry to finish up. With the door wide open for all to see, she sits in full view of the road taunting passing motorists in need of a place of relief. This comical outhouse is part of a bizarre decorative menagerie on someone's front lawn in the wilds of Wisconsin.

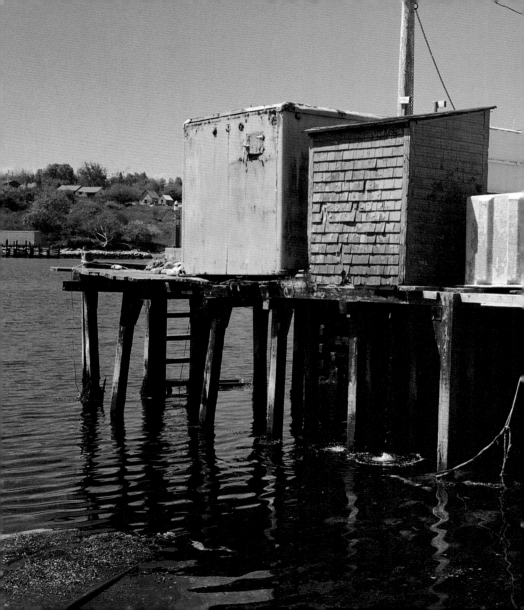

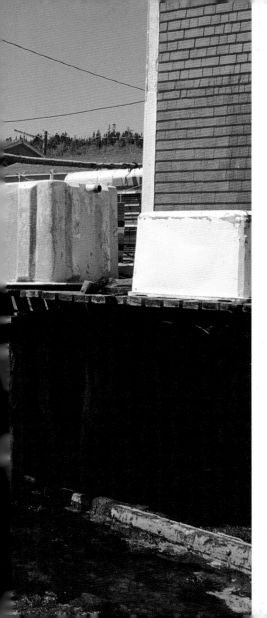

**North West Cove
Blanford Peninsula
Lunenburg County
Nova Scotia**

Federal government public wharfs such as this are often found in the quaint coves of Nova Scotia. The small rust-coloured building in the middle is a two-seater outhouse moved to the wharf by the local fishermen. Several planks have been removed from under it for easy evacuation into the shallow water below, a practice of which the environmentally conscious government is certainly unaware.

USS *Pampanito*
Pier 45
Fisherman's Wharf
San Francisco
California

Using the toilet on a submarine is a complicated business. With twenty men per toilet, the 'heads' on the World War II USS *Pampanito* were busy places. To use, turn the red valve above the toilet and the bowl will fill with water. When the bowl is half full, stop the flow of water by turning the valve off. The head is now ready for use. When finished, lift and lower the red lever at the base of the toilet to flush. When the time comes to empty the contents of the sewage tank, great care must be taken to ensure that all valves in the submarine are closed. Failure to do so will result in a high-pressure explosion of sewage throughout the submarine at a force of 225 pounds per square inch.

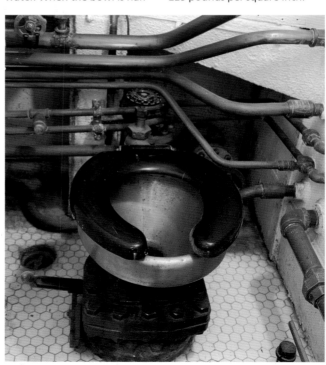

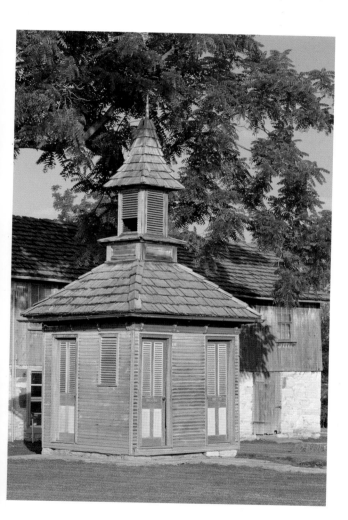

**Tulpehocken Manor
Route 422
Myerstown
Lebanon County
Pennsylvania**

President George Washington was the most illustrious user of this attractive 1700s manor outhouse. He allegedly resided here as a guest at least once in the late eighteenth century. Interestingly for this period, there were separate sides for men and women. The women's side was more spacious, to allow room for cumbersome hoop dresses. There was also a much shorter bench with a small hole for children. Ancient by American standards, the outhouse and adjacent home have been lovingly restored.

41

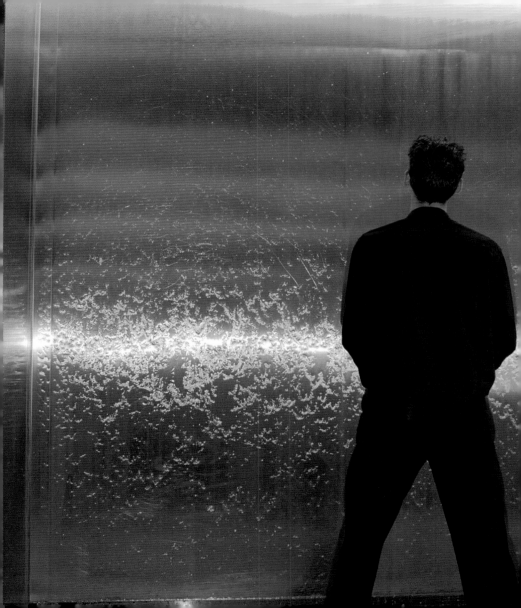

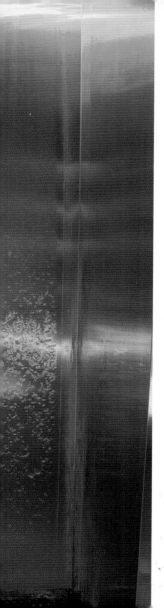

Whiskey Café
5800 Blvd St Laurent
Montréal
Québec

During the course of an
evening spent sampling the
seventy varieties of whisky
available in this Montréal
café, a trip to the toilet is
inevitable. Activated by
sensors, this massive metal
urinal fills an entire wall. A
stream of water flows down
its face while it is being used
and shuts off when the user
leaves. To relieve oneself
legally on such a large
expanse of steel in a public
place is a rare treat. The
soothing ambient lighting
contributes to the whole
satisfying experience.

New England Air Museum
Bradley International
Airport
Windsor Locks
Connecticut

The toilet takes on a whole new dimension when it comes to outer space. This high-tech toilet is the prototype for that on the International Space Station. Years of meticulous research have gone into our astronauts' facilities for what is no longer a mundane daily act – gravity has never been taken for granted more than when it comes to the toilet.

Astronauts must strap on to the toilet, as sealing the seat is of utmost importance in a zero-gravity environment. A complicated vacuum system is incorporated under the seat, where liquid and solid matter must be dealt with separately. Since no one is certain of the consequences of ejecting solid waste into space, it is compressed into round, flat discs, referred to by NASA's toilet engineers as 'people patties'. These are brought back to earth for two reasons: for the lucky lab technician whose job it is to analyse them, and to avoid the possibility of a solid-waste asteroid hurtling towards the earth.

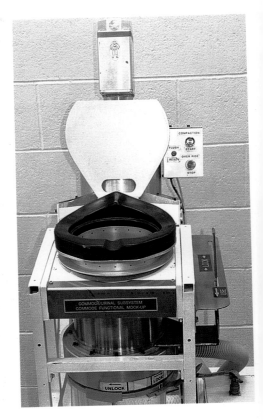

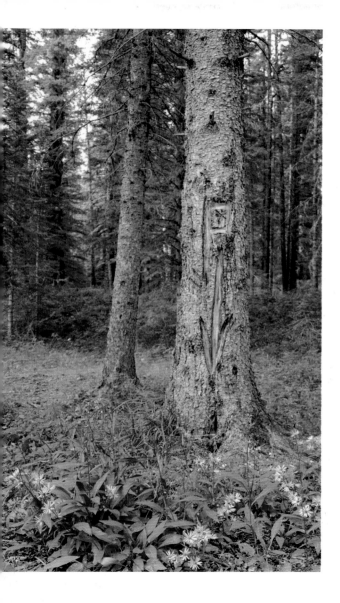

Forestry Trunk Road
Red Deer River
near Sundre
Alberta

No Canadian campsite would be complete without its own pee tree. Usually found wherever a makeshift campsite is set up, pee trees can also be useful in official campgrounds when the latrines are an uncomfortable distance away. The purpose of the pee tree is self-explanatory. Using the pee tree promotes the theory behind camping: to exist without the modern conveniences we take for granted in an effort to come closer to nature.

45

DNA Lounge
375 Eleventh Street
San Francisco
California

In a nightclub context, these angular chrome urinals on black tile walls are chic and modern. They are far less glamorous in their intended setting. These are prison-issue urinals, manufactured specifically for jails across America.

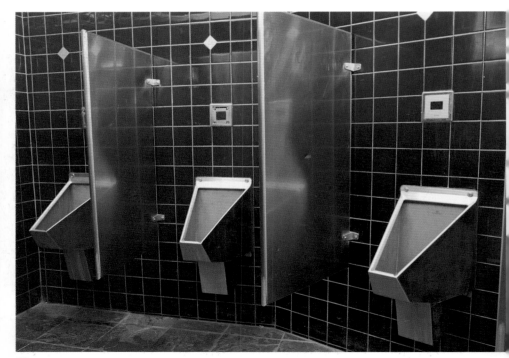

Johnston Canyon Resort
Bow Valley Parkway
Banff National Park
Alberta

Although the water-saving selective flusher has been common in other parts of the world for quite some time, it has been surprisingly slow in making its appearance in North America. The user has a choice of two flushes according to need. The smaller button uses a reduced amount of water, while the other flushes the standard volume. The photograph is rather explicit: liquid/wee wee needs a little flush and solid/doo doo needs a regular-sized flush.

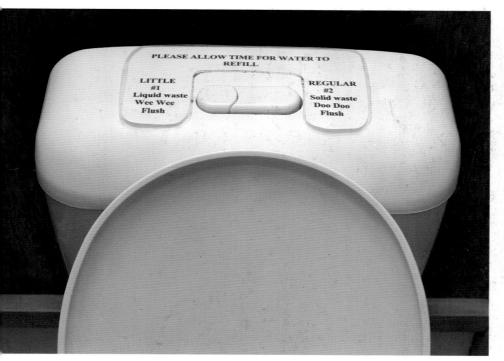

PLEASE ALLOW TIME FOR WATER TO REFILL

LITTLE
#1
Liquid waste
Wee Wee
Flush

REGULAR
#2
Solid waste
Doo Doo
Flush

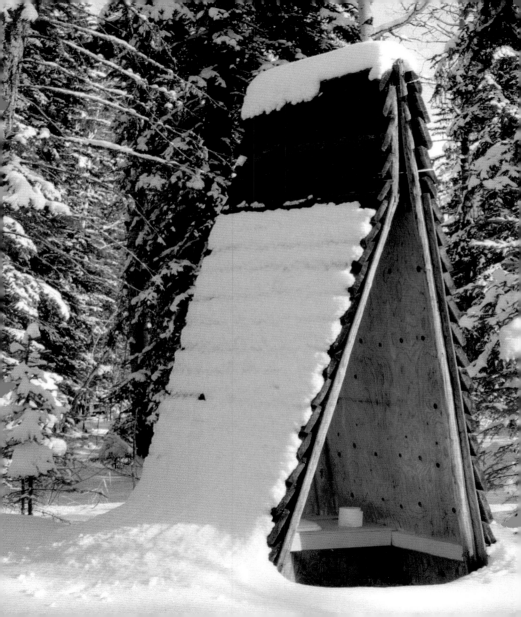

Terratima Lodge
Rocky Mountain House
Alberta

One can contemplate the
pristine Canadian wilderness
while seated in this doorless
A-frame outhouse on the
edge of the Rocky Mountains.
But do not contemplate too
long – when temperatures
drop to a frigid forty below,
bare skin freezes in less than
thirty seconds. Common in
snowy climates, the A-frame
structure prevents the
accumulation of heavy snow
that causes roofs to collapse.

Canada

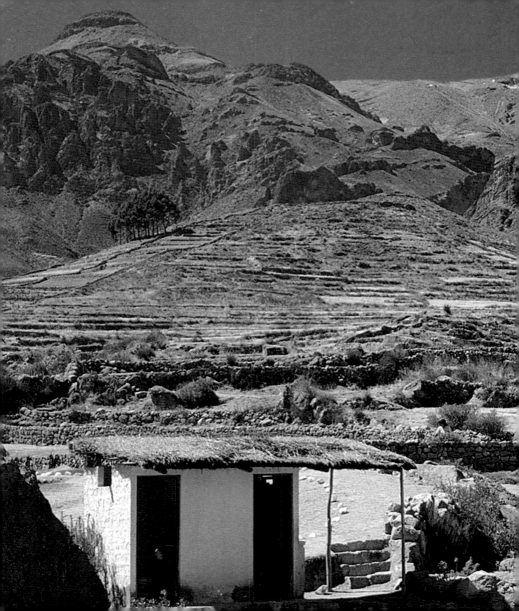

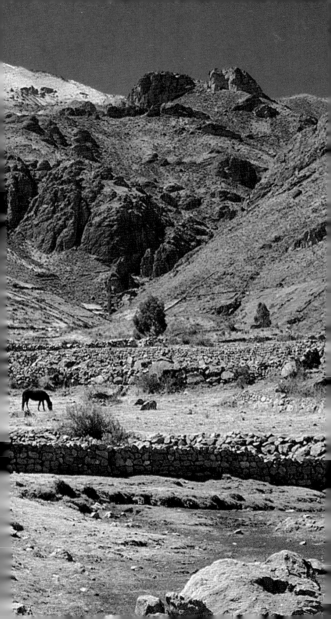

Evidence of the Spanish conquistadores co-exists with the surviving traditions of the ancient indigenous peoples throughout Central and South America. The influences of both are everywhere and are staple features of the topography from the Andes to the Amazon. Town squares abound with stately colonial architecture while ancient ruins look down over fallen empires from the surrounding hillsides. This part of the New World evokes images of jungles, mountains, oceans, cocaine, parrots, mines, llamas and improbable feats of engineering. As if these were not enough, Central and South America have their own unique toilets waiting to be sniffed out by those in search of the most basic necessity of Latin American culture.

Although many of the native languages survived the Spanish invasion, the continent is largely Spanish speaking. Public toilets, called *baños* or *servicios*, are not rare in areas of high pedestrian traffic in the southern Americas. A few Brazilian reals, Costa Rican colones, Chilean pesos or Bolivian bolivianos will buy a visit to the *servicios públicos*. After paying the cashier and own. The adobe outhouse is found across the cordillera, for both private and communal use. They are built of home-made bricks moulded from the local soil. The privies behind private homes usually have a roof, but communal ones almost never do. For many an Andean family, this is the toilet they have always known and likely always will. Communal adobe outhouses are found behind remote mountain schoolhouses or in places tourists might visit, such as lakes or hot springs. These durable toilets are short square structures with a hole dug into the ground.

Toilets often exist in adaptation to the surrounding environment, as exemplified by the facilities used by certain coastal peoples. The Kuna Indians of the San Blas region of Panama, for example, utilize the action of the Caribbean tides rather than worry about the logistics of plumbing. To reach their unique toilets, the Kuna walk a rickety plank out across the water to reach the *servicio* on stilts. Everything plummets into the sea below and eventually floats away on the tide.

Toilets of South America can also have a deadly side.

The most notorious cocaine mogul the world has ever known, Colombian Pablo Escobar Gaviria, had a self-destructive relationship with Latin loos. Although fully at ease with gruesome assassinations, the wealthy drug lord had an overpowering phobia of dirty toilets. Escobar's throne was for his use only and was cleaned three times a day, every day. While on the run, he was forced to forsake his mansions to live in dilapidated hideouts. A trail of shabby houses with impeccably clean and modern bathrooms led the authorities to make the bust of their lives. They flushed him out and shot him on the spot.

Like the jewels buried in their mines, exquisite Latin American toilets lie awaiting discovery. Among these gems are cactus toilets, toilets in sinks, ghost-town toilets, and outhouses surveyed by condors. From a unique perspective, toilets tell tales of the diverse people and landscapes of Central and South America.

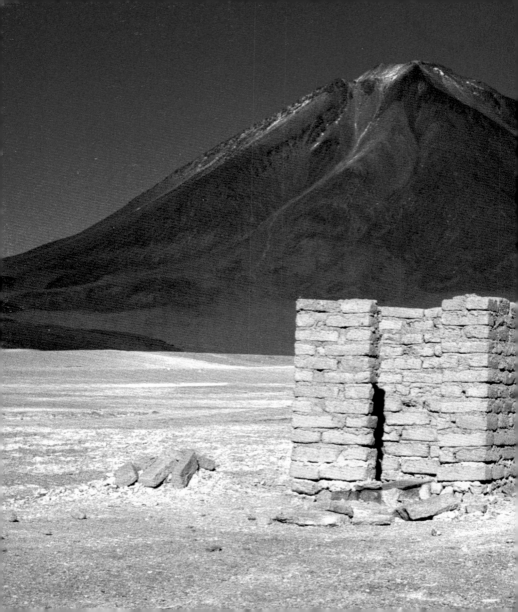

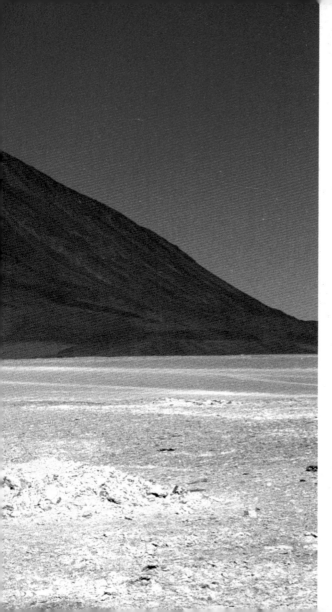

Lincanabur Volcano
South-western Cordillera
High Andes

A dizzying 5900 metres (19,300 ft) above sea level at its crater, this imposing volcano straddles the border between Bolivia and Chile. The air at the short stone toilet below is so thin that its users are advised not to overexert themselves to avoid altitude sickness. The toilet serves the nearby Termas de Polques hot springs, where brave visitors to this barren landscape can escape the icy Andean winds by immersing themselves in the steaming water bubbling up from the earth.

55

Yanque
Colca Canyon
Departamento de Arequipa

Travellers to Peru's Colca Canyon visit this Andean village to admire its spectacular Spanish colonial church. The locals along the main road have exploited the tourist trade by opening toilets for public use. This Quechua woman in her traditional clothing collects a small fee for the use of her facilities, which come as something of a surprise. Once through a dilapidated courtyard and a rickety wooden door, the inside of the facility shimmers like an oasis with a brand new, fully plumbed white sparkling throne.

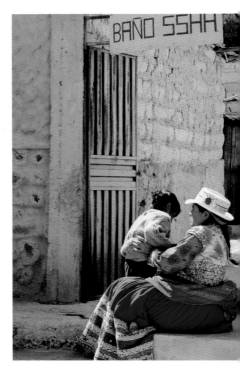

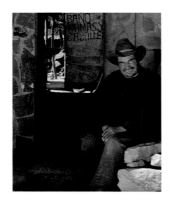

Further up the Yanque main road, this man collects Peruvian soles for the use of his toilet.

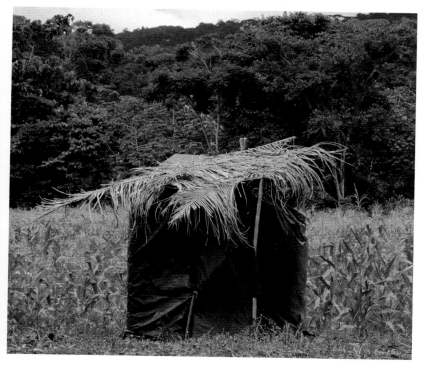

Squatter Settlement
Drake's Bay
Peninsula de Osa

In an attempt to improve standards of hygiene, the Costa Rican government distributed moulded plastic toilets to people in remote areas. The idea was to encourage the peasants to install septic tanks. In most cases, the toilets have simply been placed over the existing hole in the ground. Such is the case of this toilet. Overlooking a cornfield and the distant mountains, the outhouse is made with sheets of plastic and a roof of palm branches.

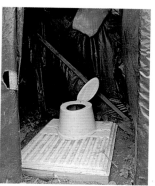

A moulded plastic toilet placed in a basic outhouse.

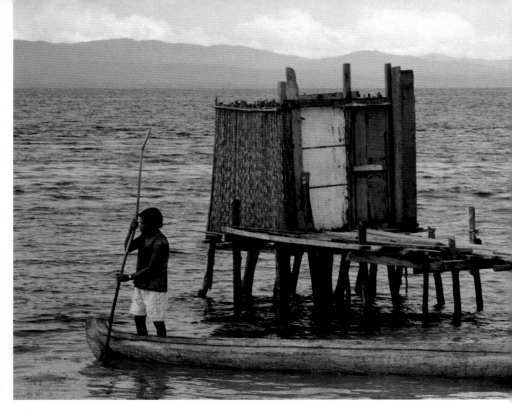

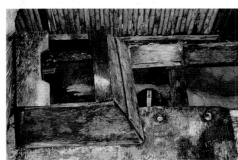

An unsuspecting snorkeller swims right under the toilet.

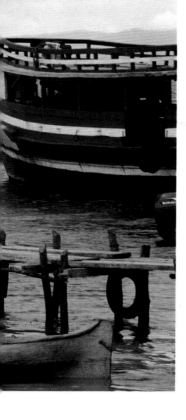

Nalunega Island
San Blas Archipelago

A Kuna man glides past the toilet in his boat carved from a palm-tree trunk while a Colombian trading vessel is anchored behind. The Kuna Indians have had a trading agreement with Colombia for several decades using their principal form of currency: the coconut.

Naive tourists can sometimes be seen snorkelling through the docks, much to the delight of the local children. Shrieks of laughter can be heard clear across the island when the light-skinned swimmer sees the purpose of these huts on stilts. Since 90% of the archipelago's 400 islands are uninhabited, snorkelling is best reserved for cleaner waters.

59

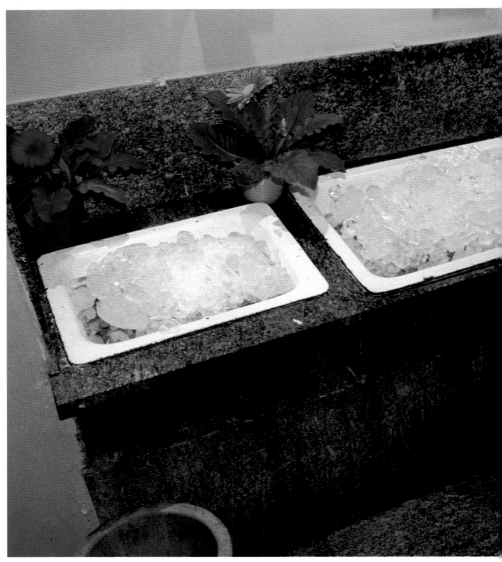

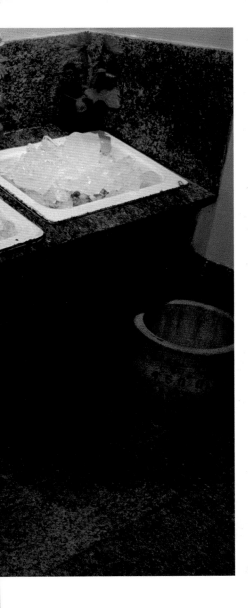

Marius
Avenida Atlântica 290
Leme Beach
Rio de Janeiro

Three old cast-iron sinks, set
lower than normal, serve as
the urinals in this upscale
restaurant. This alone makes
for an intriguing image, but it
is their contents that make
these urinals truly unique. At
the bottom of each sink is a
thick layer of stones, upon
which a layer of ice cubes is
poured every evening. The
rationale for using ice in
urinals is to eliminate odours,
though this practice is far, far
less effective than chemicals.

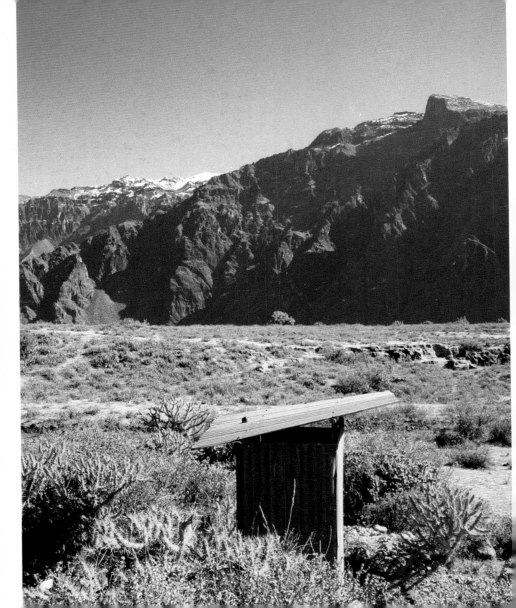

Cruz del Condor
Colca Canyon
Caylloma
Departamento de Arequipa

This corrugated-steel
outhouse is guarded by
Andean cacti on the edge of
the Colca Canyon. Twice the
depth of the Grand Canyon,
it is the deepest on earth.
This is the domain of the
rare Andean condor, often
seen rising on the morning
thermals above this outhouse.
With a wingspan of more
than 3 metres (9 ft), the
Andean condor is the largest
flying bird in the world.

Peru

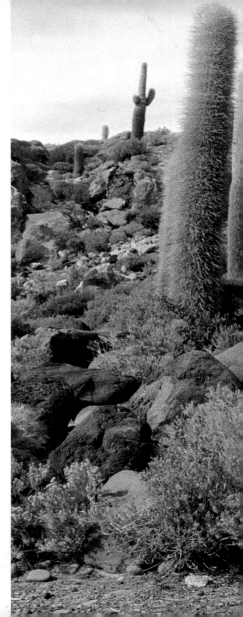

Incahuasi Island
Uyuni Salt Flats
Altiplano Boliviano

Straight out of a surreal painting, this 'island' covered in giant cacti is in the middle of an astonishing 12,000 square kilometre (4600 square mile) salt desert. On the remote Bolivian high plateau things are often made of the materials at hand. This toilet was carved from the trunk of a dried cactus, which is the only abundant material here other than salt. For comfort's sake, all its needles have been removed. Situated along the hiking trail that circles the island, this toilet sits over a hole dug in the ground.

The Uyuni salt desert.

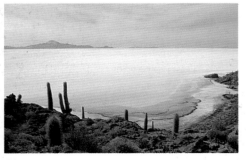

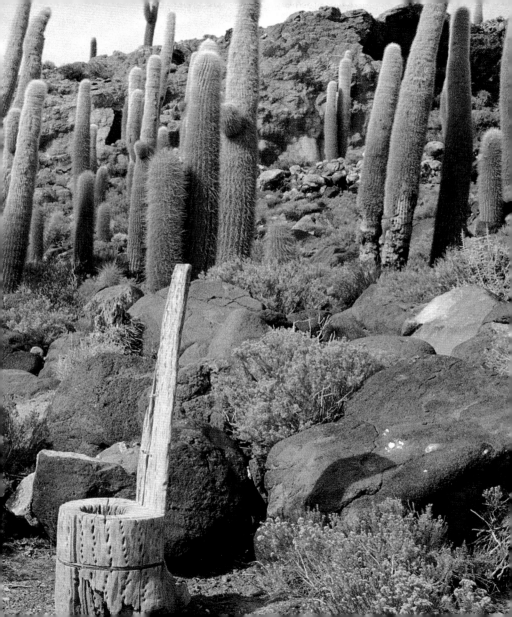

Humberstone
Route 16
45 km (28 miles) east
of Iquique
Atacama Desert

The Atacama Desert is the driest on earth, boasting areas that have never recorded rainfall. The town of Humberstone, situated just off the Pan-American Highway, sprang up out of the sand after the discovery of lucrative saltpetre veins in the nineteenth century. The nitrate extracted here was shipped worldwide to be used as fertilizer and in the making of explosives.

In its turn-of-the-century heyday, the town had 3700 residents. Humberstone thrived for decades as one of the most important nitrate excavations in South America, until it was deserted almost overnight in 1960 after the invention of synthetic nitrate. The town is extremely well preserved, although it is slowly eroding away under the blistering desert sun.

The mayor had a more
extravagant house.
This was his spacious toilet,
complete with tiled flooring.

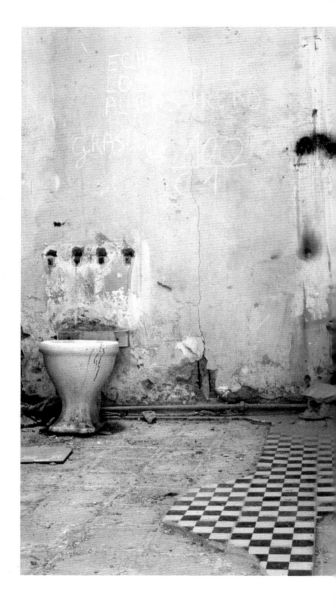

schoolhouse toilet in the ghost town of umberstone.

The mining labourers and their families lived in simple row houses. Each house had a toilet identical to this one.

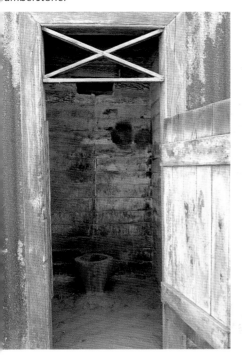

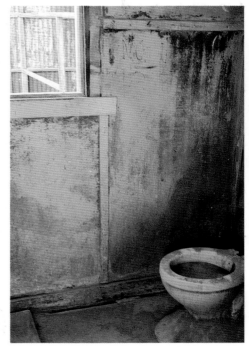

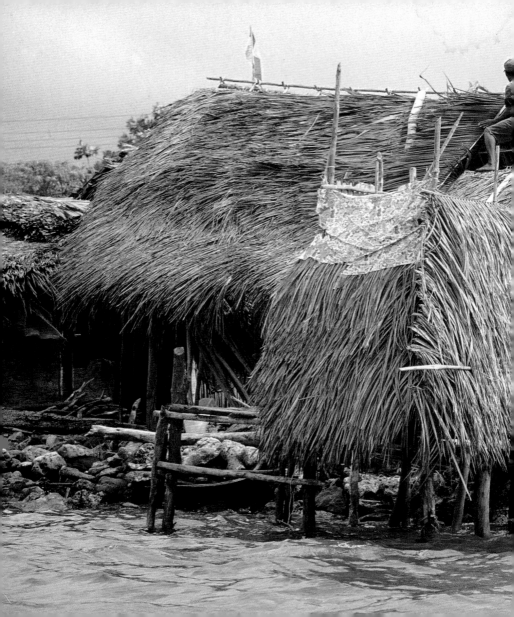

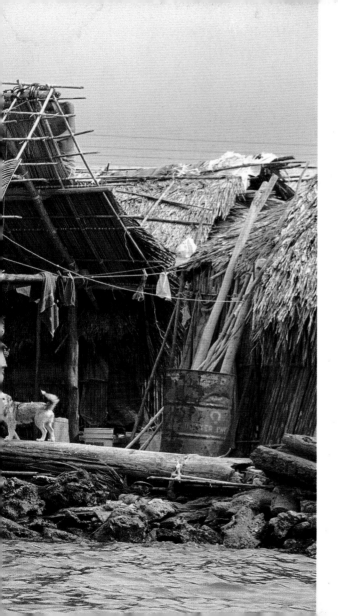

Isla Cartí Suitupo
San Blas Archipelago

Only the size of three football fields, the tiny island of Cartí Suitupo is inhabited by more than 2000 people. Every imaginable variety of the Kuna toilet protrudes from the entire circumference of Cartí. Of all colours, sizes and materials, a multitude of planks and docks with their tiny huts stretches out over the water like so many spider legs. This toilet is made of thatched palm leaves, the same material that is being used to roof the house. Twice daily, the tide faithfully sweeps the aftermath of Cartí's zealous toilet use out to sea or to neighbouring Kuna islands.

69

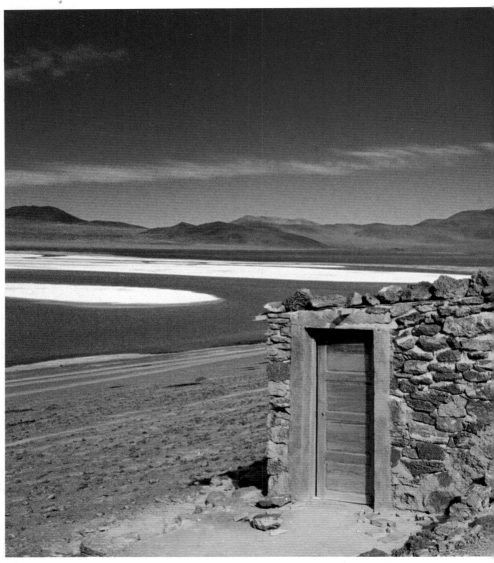

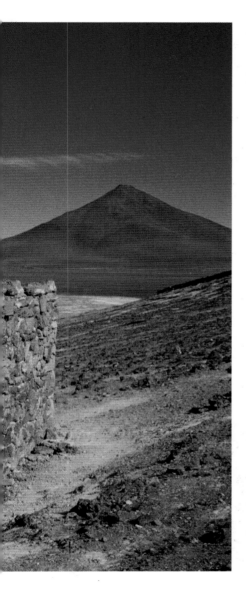

Laguna Colorada
Eduardo Avaroa Andean
Fauna National Reserve
Sud Lipez

The largest lake of the Andean high plateau gets its deep crimson colour from the algae that thrive in its mineral-rich waters. Without the pigments in the algae, the flamingos that feed here would be entirely white. The simple brick toilet overlooking the lake is relatively recent. It was built for adventurers who brave the hostile climate to experience the region's ethereal landscapes. Below, scattered herds of llama graze on the scrub grass. The chalky white shoreline is rich in borax, used to make detergent and ceramics, and to disintegrate rust.

The threatened James's flamingos feed on algae, which will change their colour to pink.

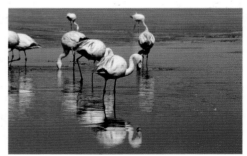

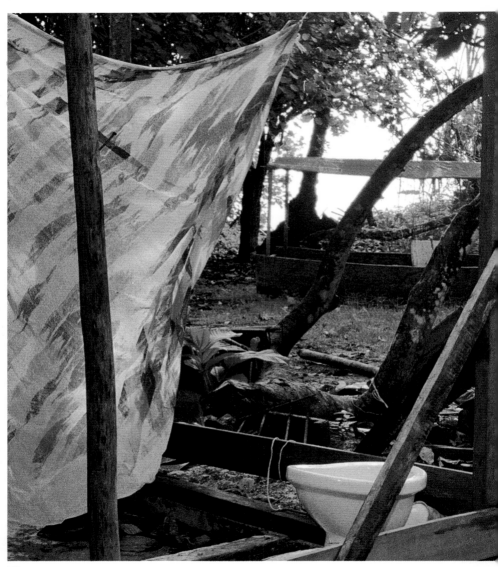

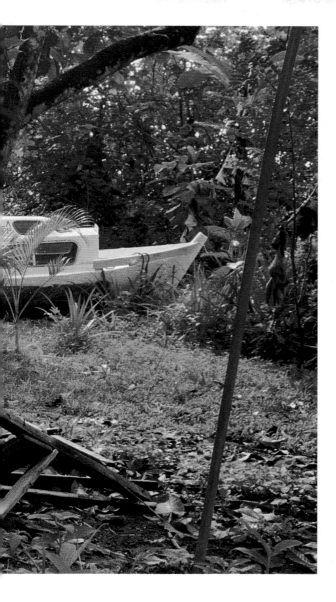

Drake's Bay
Península de Osa

The cabin of the boat in the background is home to a tiny ancient woman. Her toilet is modern and kept impeccably clean. It appears as though someone intended to build a structure around the porcelain fixture, but so far there is only a basic wooden frame placed on the cement foundation. Meanwhile, a shower curtain has been hung for privacy.

Near Chivay
Colca Canyon
Departamento de Arequipa

High in the Peruvian Andes, this toilet is an oasis for the squat-weary trekker. These are the public facilities of a remote mountain restaurant.

Incredibly, the clean flush toilets are equipped with modern plumbing and are connected to an efficient septic tank. Pre-Columbian Inca agricultural terraces line the mountainside. The nearby ponds are teeming with feisty Peruvian rainbow trout for a tasty catch-it-yourself lunch.

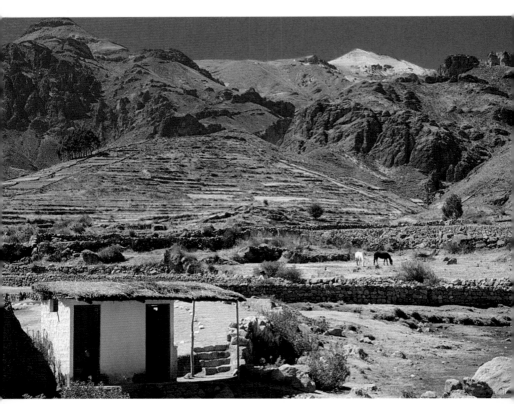

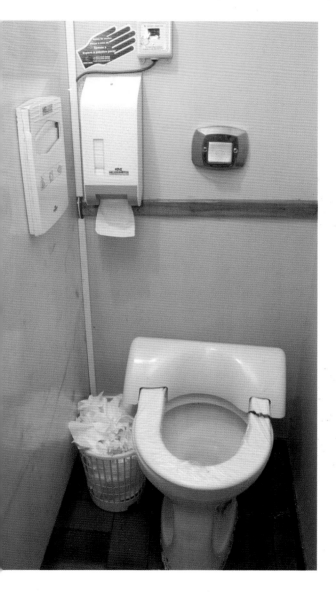

La Trattoria
Rua Fernando Mendez 7
Copacabana
Rio de Janeiro

Although unremarkable at first glance, this cubicle is ironically hilarious. Note the obsession with seat cleanliness: not only does the seat have an automated plastic covering that is renewed with each flush, but there is also a seat cover dispenser on the wall for those suffering from extreme germ wariness. Bacteriophobes will also be pleased to note the touchless flushing sensor. But then, much to their horror, there is an unhygienic mountain of dirty toilet paper next to the nicely sanitized seat. In much of Brazil the plumbing technology is not as advanced as seat protection technology. Used paper must be thrown in the garbage rather than flushed away.

75

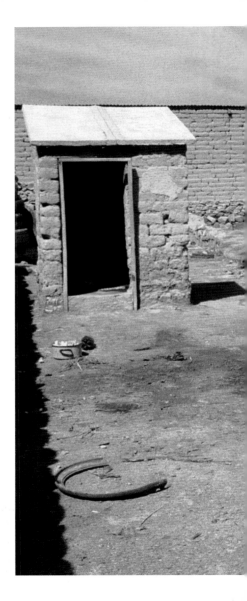

**Colchani
Departamento
de Cochabamba**

A dusty, windswept desert
village of fewer than 200
people, Colchani ekes out an
existence with the extraction
of salt. The vast, barren salt
flats begin on the outer edge
of the village. There is no
plumbing or electricity and
time stood still many decades
ago. This family's rustic toilet
stands in their backyard, with
a few rusted trucks and other
unidentified machinery. Like
this outhouse, the adobe
buildings of Colchani are the
colour of the Sud Lipez desert
and are being whittled away
by the harsh winds of the
high plateau.

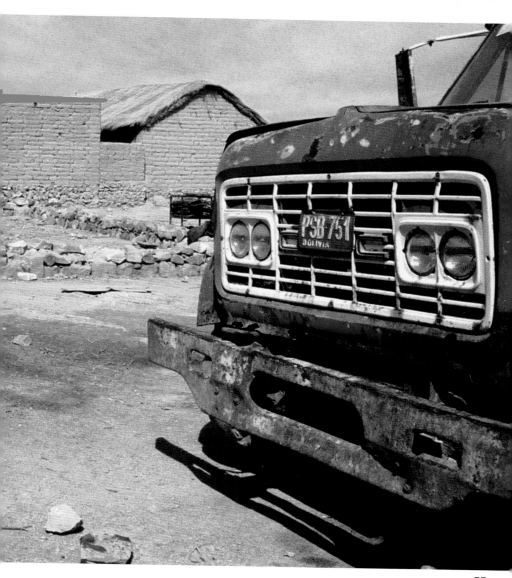

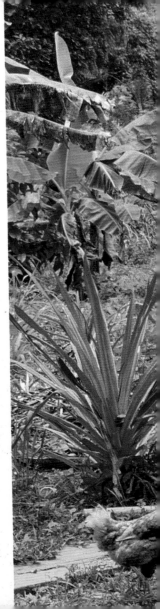

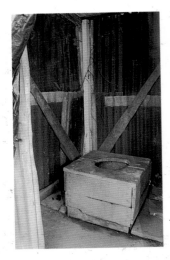

Squatter Settlement
Drake's Bay
Peninsula de Osa

A wealthy farmer had the unpleasant surprise of discovering that by law, in Costa Rica, land uninhabited for more than thirty days becomes fair game. During his absence, squatters moved in on the farmer's vast land and numerous farmhouses and took ownership. Legal questions aside, most interesting toilets have been constructed by the squatters. This one was slapped up with whichever materials were at hand. Chickens often have to be shooed out of this backyard family toilet.

A wooden box forms the toilet inside this outhouse.

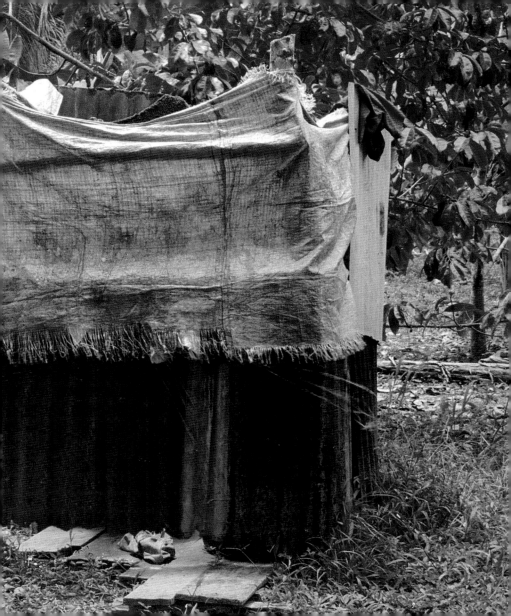

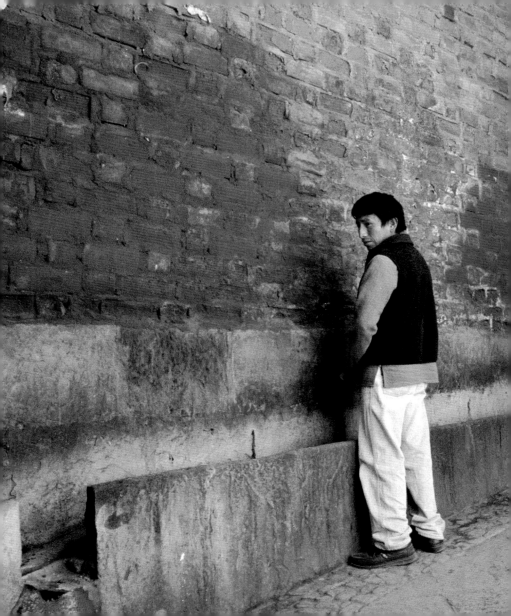

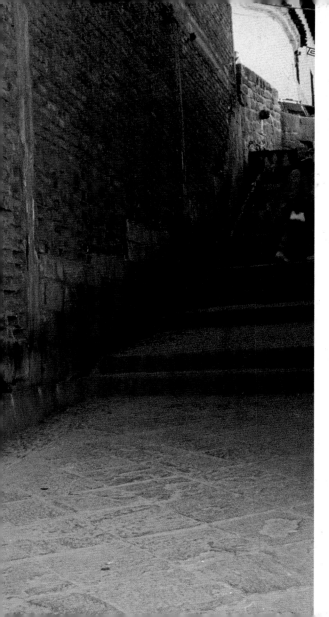

Avenida Tullumayo
Cuzco

The fountain at the very top of the stairs is the source of this massive open urinal. Water runs through a gutter along the stairs, down the alley and finally into a drain below. Local women are often seen holding their bare-bottomed children over it. Like most inhabitants of Cuzco, the user seen here is a Quechua Indian and descendant of the ancient Incas. Said to be the oldest living city in the Americas, Cuzco was the capital of the great Inca civilization and is now the tourists' gateway to Machu Picchu. A search for ancient Inca toilets proved fruitless – the people simply used their cornfields.

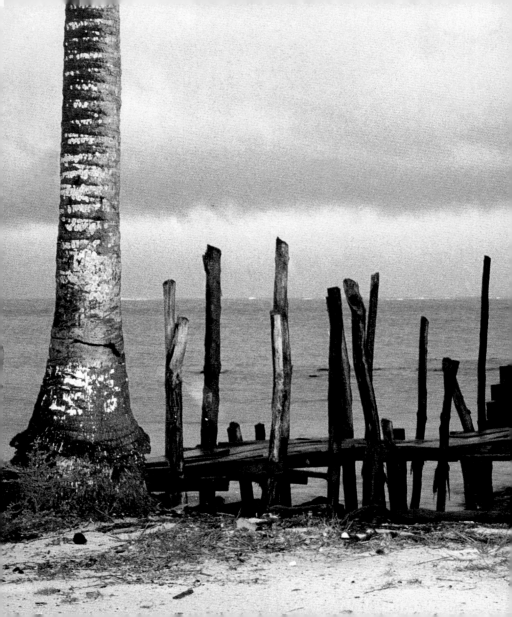

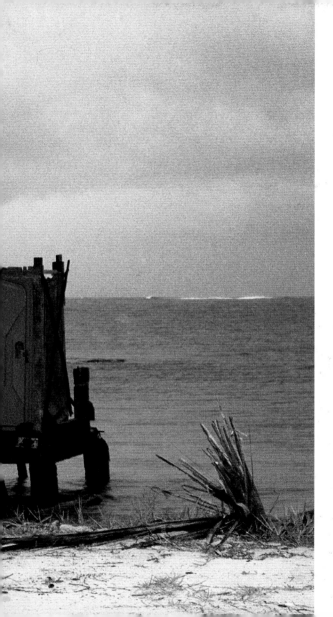

El Porvenir airport
San Blas Archipelago

The toilet of Panama's
El Porvenir airport is
definitely not suitcase-
friendly or wheelchair-
accessible. As in the case
of most toilets in the San
Blas Archipelago, users are
required to negotiate a
narrow plank across the
water to reach the toilet on
stilts. Perhaps in an effort to
install a facility somewhat
recognizable to foreigners,
the Kuna have utilized an
old blue porta-potty. No
chemicals or pump-trucks are
needed here though: what
goes in falls straight through
to the sea below.

Nalunega Island
San Blas Archipelago

Patiently waiting her turn, this Kuna woman is brightly dressed in her daily traditional garb of embroidery and leg beads. Her son is inside the *servicio*, squealing with glee as he aims at the fish below. This toilet is made of wood and concrete blocks, and the family is fortunate to have a dock rather than a rickety two-by-four to take them to their suspended facility.

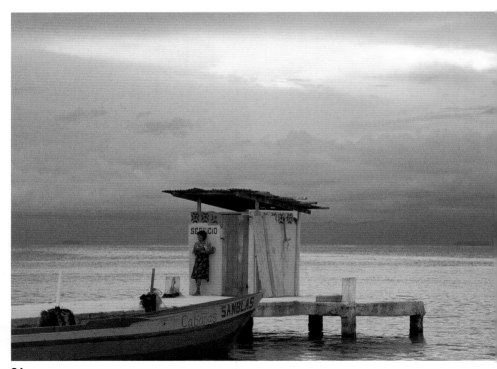

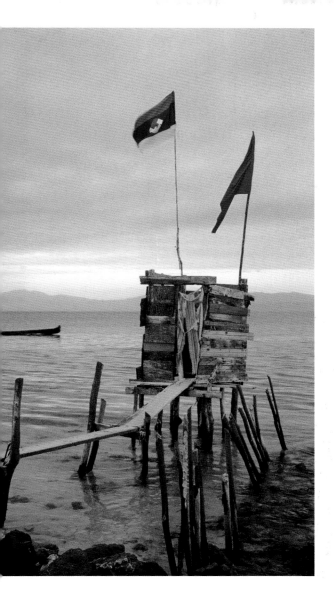

Nalunega Island
San Blas Archipelago

Even in the twenty-first century, the Kuna Indians have preserved the traditional culture of their ancestors. This is reflected in the construction of their toilets, simple huts on stilts above the crystalline waters of the Caribbean. Belonging to the island's chief, this toilet sports two flags representing opposing Panamanian political parties. Perhaps the purpose of the flags – unless they are purely decorative – is to reflect the autonomous status of the Kuna in Panama.

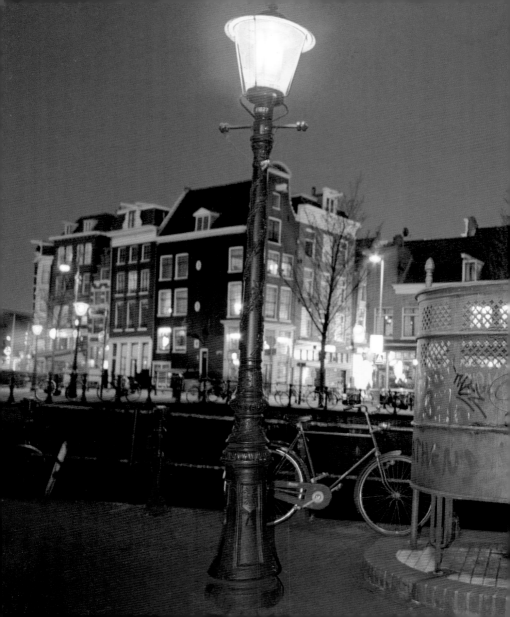

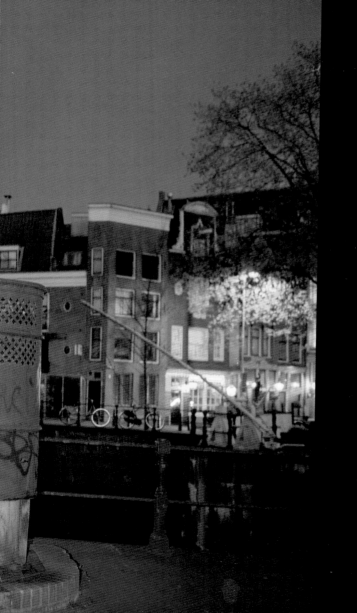

Ask anyone familiar with Europe to talk about the variety of toilets encountered there, and the discussion frequently leads to hours of surreal descriptions and anecdotes. Europe is truly a wealth of astonishing facilities, from fully automated toilets to strange and frightening holes in the floor. Public toilets along busy city streets and open-air urinals on town squares are all banal. European men have few qualms about relieving themselves in public, regardless of others in the vicinity. In pubs women regularly have to walk past men using the urinals before reaching a private stall. Finding the toilet is always a mission as one climbs up or down stairs, goes outside, down the alley or across the parking lot, or feels the way along a tiny dark corridor. Even the normally thoughtless act of flushing suddenly becomes a great challenge to the foreigner, who is forever in search of something to push, pull, knee, touch, twist, crank or stomp on.

Like many cultural attractions in Europe, a visit to the toilet is often subject to an entrance fee. Although a permanent source of irritation to overseas visitors, paying to piddle is common.

Payment is made in one of two ways. Many pay toilets are coin-operated, as is often the case of the modern public toilet booths found on streets in large cities. Coin-operated stalls are also current in train stations and various other public venues.

The second way to pay is just as infuriating but at least evokes a certain fascination. One must hand a coin to the 'pee lady'. She is known by a variety of names depending on the local language: in France she is 'Madame Pipi' and to the Germans she is 'Klofrau'. She sits at a table at the entrance to the toilets with her plate full of coins. In return for payment, the pee lady hands out toilet paper if it's not already present in the stalls. She also ensures the cleanliness of the premises, often wiping the seat after each use. In bars and nightclubs, she charges per visit, regardless of how often the patron requires her services. Note that although commonly thought of as the pee lady, the pee man is not entirely unknown.

An introduction to the toilet of Europe would be incomplete without a mention of squats. Found throughout much of the world, squat toilets are surprisingly common in France and southern Europe. The first time an uninitiated user stumbles into one of these it is always a traumatic but memorable experience. Entering a stall and expecting to find a familiar toilet, one is confronted by a forbidding hole in the floor with a large porcelain footprint on each side. Facing the door with a foot on each footprint, one must carefully squat over the hole. Long-haired beginners are urged to tie up their hair before proceeding. A considerable amount of athletic ability is required to maintain position for the duration of the visit. It takes practice to cease splashing shoes and trousers, but after several trials the correct foot-to-footprint ratio is finally attained.

Before embarking on the fascinating journey of the toilets of Europe, a final note on the north–south disparity regarding toilets. This applies especially to public toilets. Bear in mind that the following is a generalization, but it seems that the further south one goes, the less important the toilet becomes. In much of northern Europe, the toilet is often as well maintained as the rest of the establishment, whether a hotel, pub or restaurant.

There is usually a reasonable ratio of toilets to clients. As one goes further south, toilets become more and more a bare necessity. In southern Europe, it is not uncommon to find an expensive, crowded restaurant with one toilet for roughly one hundred places seated – men and women combined. Don't be surprised if this sole toilet is a dirty squat toilet outside the establishment. If it is a 'normal' toilet, don't expect to find it much more inviting. Although the main decor may be chic and immaculate, the lone facility often resembles a dilapidated broom closet. Southern Europeans willingly admit that toilets are a necessary nuisance to owners and patrons alike – owners for having to install them, patrons for having to use them.

A multitude of drastically different countries jammed side by side, each with its own language, culture and history, makes Europe extremely diverse over relatively short distances. Such contrasts are naturally reflected in the toilets. Deliciously unusual facilities include waterfall urinals, toilets in eggs, urinals that pop up from the ground, cave toilets, thunderboxes, and toilets full of goldfish.

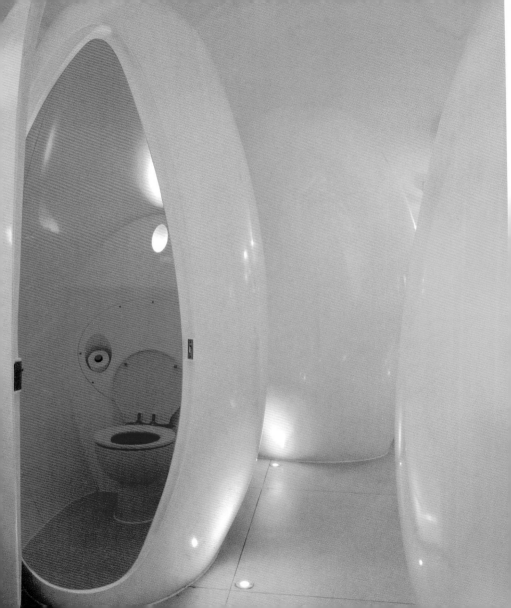

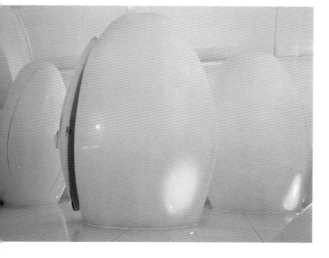

**Sketch
9 Conduit Street
London**

Many walk among these giant oblong eggs wondering if they've accidentally entered the army's restricted alien compound. When they finally crew up the courage to open the door of a forbidding egg, they realize with a gush of relief that there are no cryogenically frozen bodies inside. Instead, they find what they wanted all along: a toilet. Each of these dozen eggs contains its own perfectly normal toilet, a most relaxing little haven for all but the claustrophobic. The unique eggshells are made of fibreglass by a firm specializing in the fabrication of yacht hulls.

Pink eggs are for girls; blue eggs are for boys.

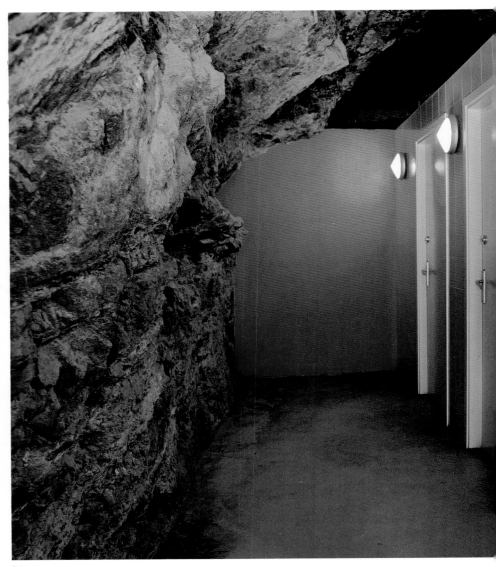

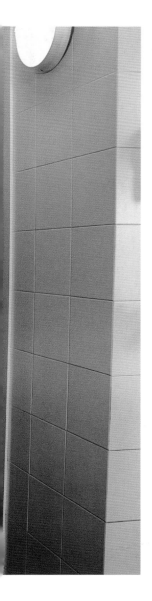

Park Güell
Barcelona
Catalonia

After a wander through the wacky park designed by Spanish architect Antonio Gaudí, these unusual toilets in a cave come as no surprise. Carved into the face of the cliff, the bathroom's rock walls have been left natural in contrast to the clean white tiles and fixtures.

Spain

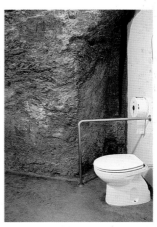

The disabled toilet in a cave.

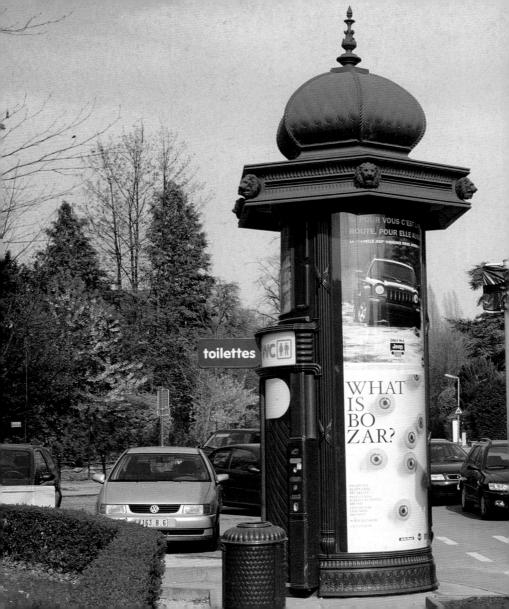

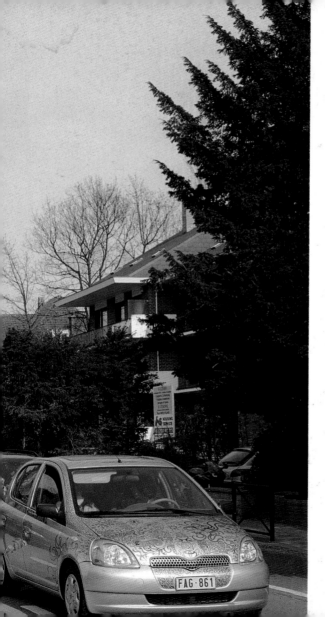

Square Maurice Raindorf
Dieweg
Uccle
Brussels

This retro-style coin-operated
public toilet also serves as an
advertisement column. It is an
example of Europe's relatively
recent efforts to compensate
for the general lack of public
toilets in cities. Inside, the
toilet itself is equipped with
a self-cleaning seat.
Bookworms be warned –
your coin buys you fifteen
minutes until the door
automatically opens.

95

**"Flushed with Pride"
Gladstone Pottery Museum
Stoke-on-Trent
Staffordshire**

Developmental problems
with early flush toilets,
including insufficient water
supply, noise and odour, led
to the creation of waterless
systems. In 1860, Reverend
Henry Moule invented the
earth closet, which consisted
of a wooden seat with a
bucket underneath. Instead
of flushing with water, a lever
was pulled and dirt, sand or
ash was released down a
funnel into the bucket to
cover up the contents. This
mixture was then dried and
used as fertilizer.

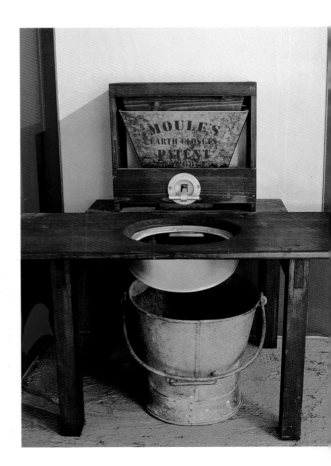

Place Emile Danco
Uccle
Brussels

Open public urinals have
been known for centuries by
French-speaking Belgians as
pissodromes or *pissoirs*. This
roofless three-man version is
made of solid marble. It is still
in use today and stands in the
middle of a busy traffic circle
surrounded by cars, shops and
pedestrians.

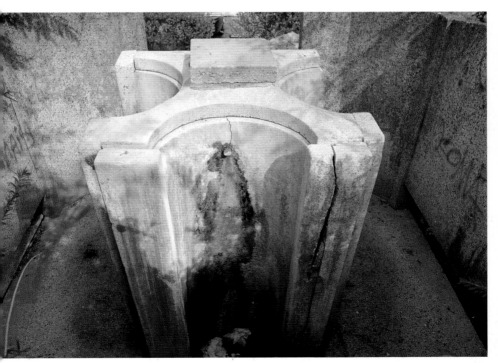

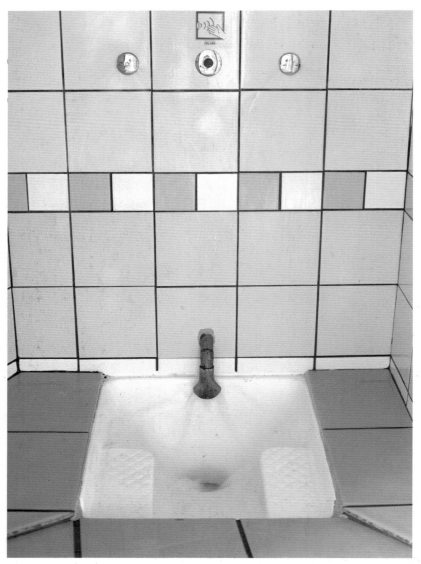

ire de Pavillion
utoroute A9
oussillon region

nown in France as a Turkish
ilet (*toilette turque*), the
uat toilet is seen here in
modern version. Facing the
or of the stall, the user
uats over the hole with
foot on each porcelain

footprint. Many find the
squat toilet more hygienic
than the classic public toilet
with a seat. Note the electric
eye on the wall: when the
user steps away, the toilet
flushes and the entire area is
automatically cleaned by a
gush of water from the three
surrounding walls.

he toilets from the outside.

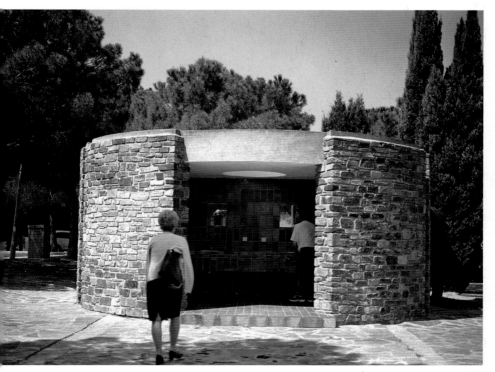

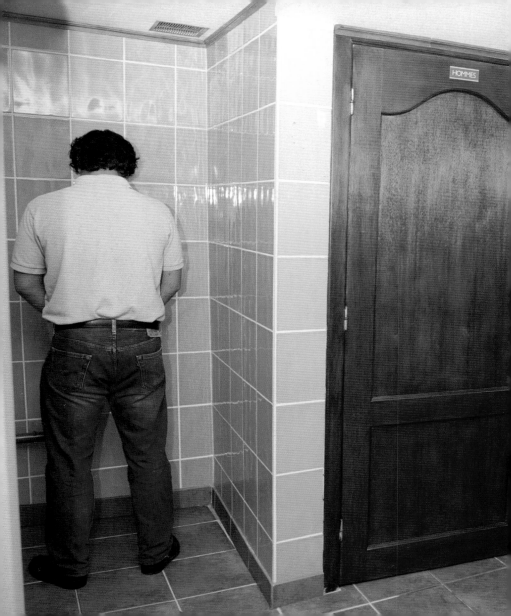

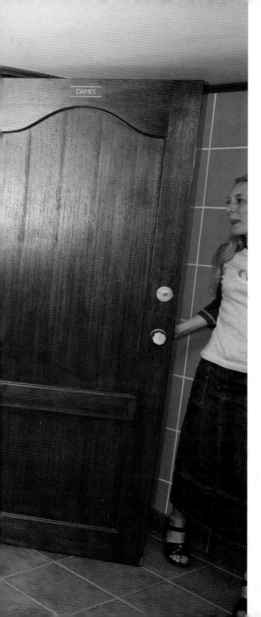

**Aux Enfants Terribles
Chaussée de la Hulpe 190
Brussels**

Many pubs and restaurants
throughout Europe have
one unisex bathroom. It is
common for women to walk
right past men busy at the
urinals before reaching a
stall. Europeans are not
bothered in the slightest
by this sharing of facilities,
which may be shocking
to many overseas visitors.

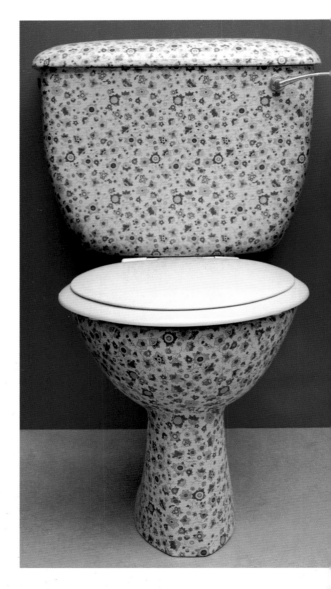

"Flushed with Pride"
Gladstone Pottery Museum
Stoke-on-Trent
Staffordshire

In the 1960s and 1970s, toilet manufacturers followed the trends of the day by making bathroom suites in shades other than the classic white. This floral toilet, described as 'tabasco'-coloured, is part of a matching set complete with sink and bathtub. The advantage of this motif is that should someone happen to vomit all over it, it would scarcely be noticeable. The popular hues of the era led to psychedelic bathroom suites in pink, yellow, orange and avocado. Groovy, baby.

102

usée Rodin
rue de Varenne
ris

Male visitors to the Rodin Museum in Paris are amused by these delightful little ball-shaped urinals. Sometimes, there is absolutely nothing to say about a toilet other than what is plainly obvious in the picture. It's cute and it's round and that's all there is to it.

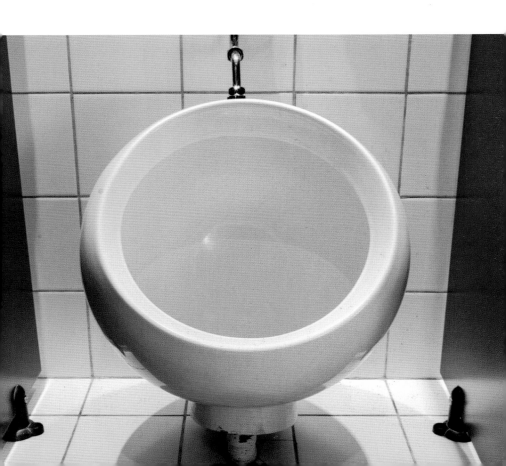

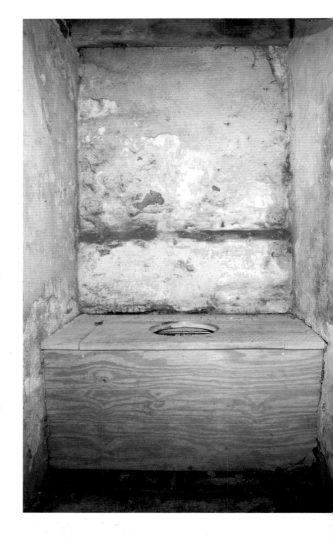

Lost Gardens of Heligan near Mevagissey Cornwall

Towards the turn of the twentieth century in rural England, toilets were typically located in a separate building outside the house. Usually hidden away in the garden, toilets were often known as 'thunderboxes' because of the sounds associated with them. This particular thunderbox was used by the gardeners who maintained the vast Heligan Estate. Waste from the toilets was collected and used to enrich the soil. At the beginning of World War I, all twenty-two gardeners enlisted, and one of them wrote on the wall of the thunderbox, "Come ye not here to sleep or slumber". Only six of the twenty-two survived the trenches of Flanders to return to their peaceful gardens.

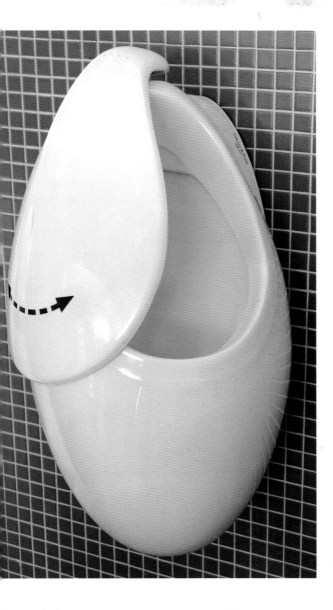

**Villeroy & Boch
Corporate Headquarters
Mettlach**

This is Oblic, the funky
space-saving urinal
developed by prestigious
housewares manufacturers
Villeroy & Boch. The small,
wall-mounted urinal has
a swivel cover over the
opening. It can be closed
when not in use by simply
sliding back the cover. The
Oblic urinal is ornamental
and decorative, yet discreet.
An aesthetic but efficient
design for wherever space
is limited.

Charing Cross Road and Shaftesbury Avenue London

Throughout the week, unsuspecting crowds in this corner of central London walk over what appears to be an oversized concrete manhole cover. On Thursdays at dusk the cover rises up from the ground to reveal a three-man urinal. Those finding themselves atop this hidden convenience needn't worry; a city worker is there to activate the facility by remote control. Catering to the male half of Soho's weekend nightlife, this part-time public relief station is one answer to the sanitary concerns faced by large cities.

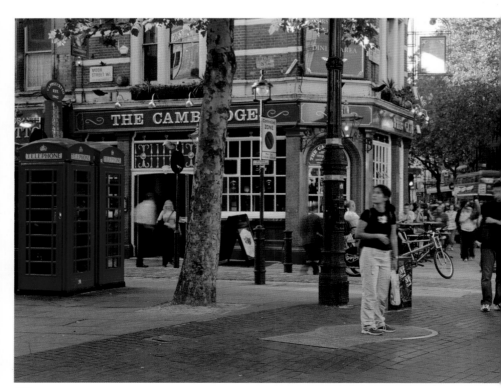

is street-corner urinal pops out of the ground every weekend.

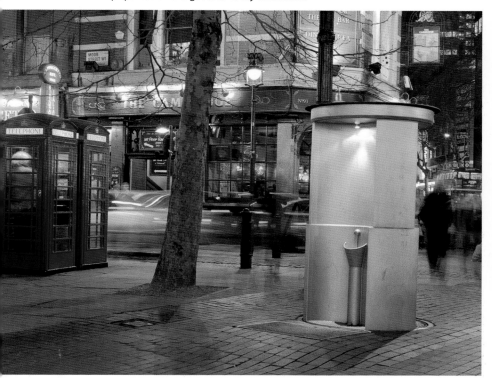

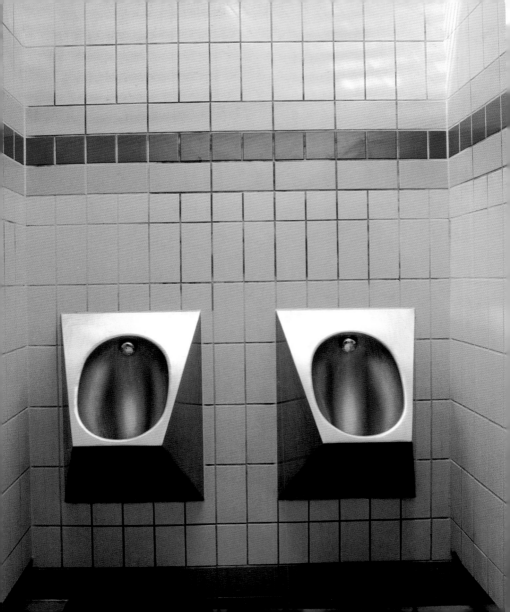

**Rastplatz Esch
Autobahn A57
near Worringen
outside Cologne**

All over the German autobahns drivers may access convenient rest stops with full toilet facilities. These stops are indicated by a blue *Rastplatz* sign, the German term for rest stop. Functionality aside, these urinals are aesthetically pleasing, with their chrome colour and the clean lines of their simple design.

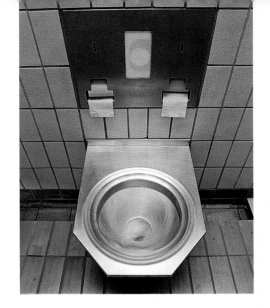

Top right: This is the typical toilet encountered in most German autobahn rest stops. The seatless toilet is flushed by touching the sensory pad located on the paper dispenser. Rastplatz *toilets and urinals are nearly always made of stainless steel.*

Bottom right: A Rastplatz *handi-loo.*

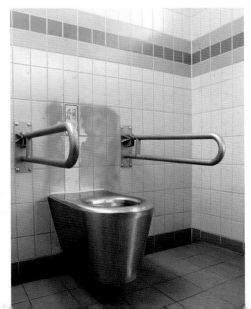

109

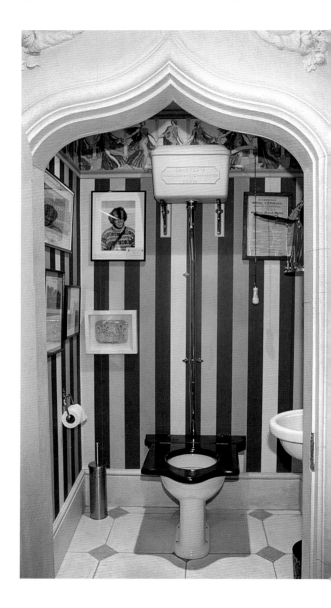

**Alscot Park Manor
Stratford-upon-Avon
Warwickshire**

In Victorian England, this model of toilet was a symbol of luxury and prestige throughout the land. It was made by the famous Thomas Crapper & Co., which has a reputation for quality that earned royal orders for its sanitary ware. Crappers of kings were installed in Buckingham Palace, Westminster Abbey and Windsor Castle. This model, the Venerable, has an elongated seat for added comfort.

110

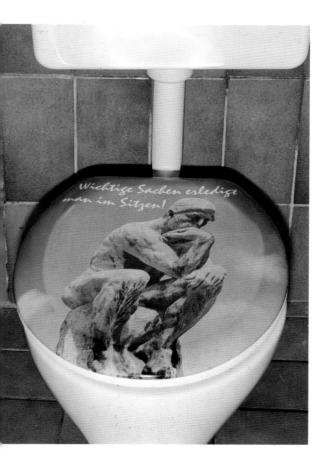

**Café-Restaurant
die Warmflasche
Berwang
Tirol**

Toilet seat manufacturers now produce decorated seats in an attempt to remain on top of an increasingly competitive market. This one depicts the French sculptor Rodin's famous bronze statue *The Thinker*. The German caption reads roughly, "Important things are best done while seated". Perhaps Rodin himself got the idea to create this statue while ... seated.

111

Thomas Crapper & Co.
The Stable Yard, Alscot Park
Stratford-upon-Avon
Warwickshire

This urinal was an ongoing private joke among the male gentry in Victorian times. There is a small bee painted into the porcelain and to the uneducated it was simply a target to aim at while using the urinal. Strategically placed targets in urinals are thought to reduce splashing. The amusement comes from the bee's Latin name: *apis*. Take apis.

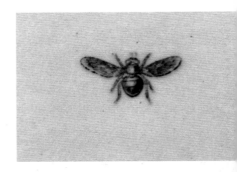

Detail of urinal showing close-up of apis.

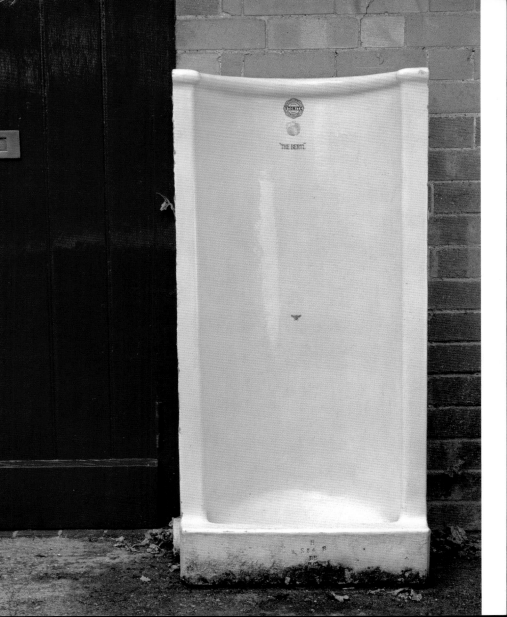

The Handelsbeurs
Borzestraat
Antwerp

Antique twin *pissijns* are found on either side of the imposing entrance to Antwerp's eighteenth-century merchants' exchange. Urinals such as these sprang up throughout cities in Belgium after the law of 1836 was passed forbidding urination in public. Although it is unusual today to see a grand entrance graced by a pair of open urinals, these are still in use and fare well owing to their solid construction of iron and marble.

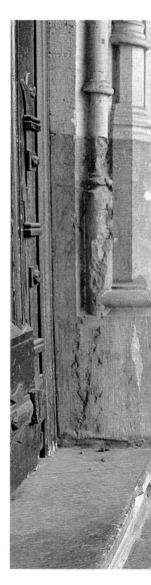

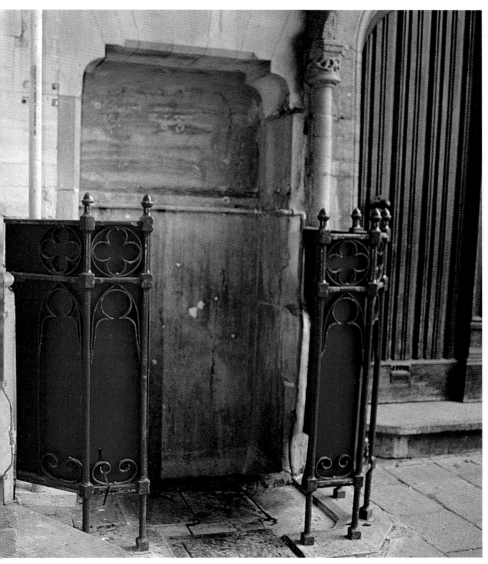

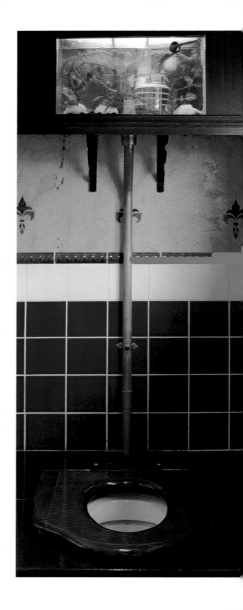

**The Crazy Bear Hotel
Stadhampton
Oxfordshire**

This original toilet tank has
been transformed into an
aquarium with live goldfish.
When the toilet is flushed,
the tank does not empty
completely. The local water
source is poor in chlorine, so
the fish thrive in a suitable
environment, but if one
happens to die its watery
grave is not far away. No fish
were harmed in the making
of these photos.

asserie Bofinger
rue de la Bastille
ris

is row of exquisite urinals
thought to have been
stalled in the 1930s, at the
ight of Paris's Art Deco
ovement. Each tall
rcelain urinal is identical,
owned with a decorative
lphin's head. They have
en used for decades by the
te of the artistic, literary
d political world. The
lphins still grace the men's
om of the first restaurant
brew its own beer, leading
e tradition of the Parisian
asserie.

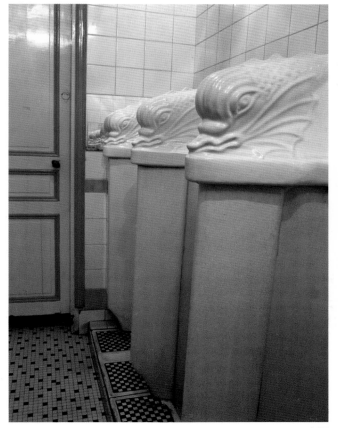

Skiana Waterski School
near Burcht
Province of Antwerp

In the Flemish region of Belgium, this rudimentary *pisbak* is fixed to the side of a shed at a waterski school. All that enters the trough flows directly into the sewage pipe in the ground below. Seasoned skiers explain to the uninitiated that it is used for washing waterskis.

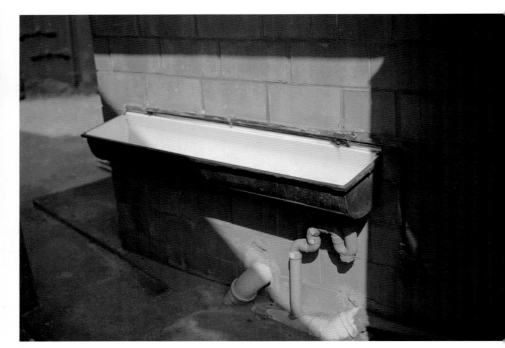

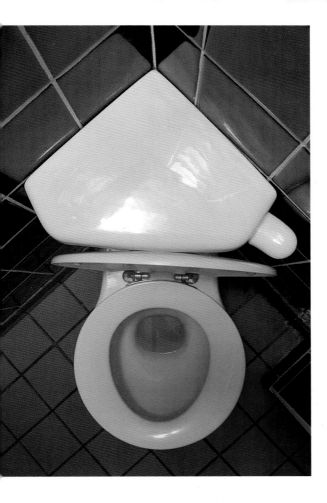

**The Ship Inn
Noss Mayo
South Hams
Devon**

In Europe, living space is not always as ample as in other parts of the world. Owing to a high population density, people are often forced to be creative with their available space. Hence the triangular corner toilet, which takes up less room than the traditional rectangular tank.

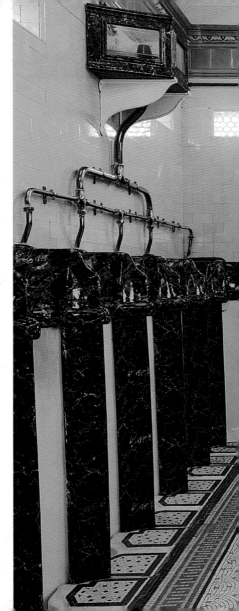

**Rothesay Pier
Isle of Bute**

These magnificent Victorian
urinals were built when
Rothesay was at the height
of its popularity as a holiday
resort. They were rescued
from demolition in 1994
when Strathclyde Building
Preservation Trust fortunately
decided to have them
renovated rather than torn
down. The total cost of
restoration work is estimated
at £300,000, compared to the
£530 it cost to build the
urinals in 1899.

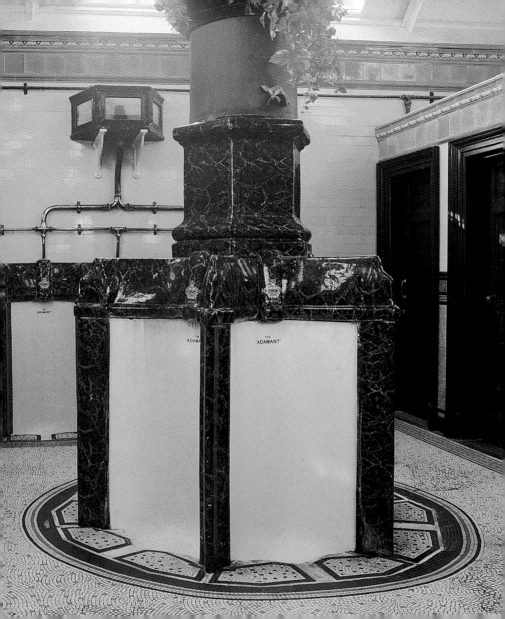

**De Notelaer
Stationsplein 2
Bornem
Flanders**

The automated self-cleaning CWS CleanSeat is a revolutionary version of the common toilet. As on a dishwasher, there is a panel on the toilet tank with coloured lights that flash in sequence to show the current phase of the cleaning cycle. Meanwhile, a mechanical device pops out of the lower part of the tank, grips the seat and spins it all the way around as it cleans and disinfects. The stylish bowl is designed by Philippe Starck.

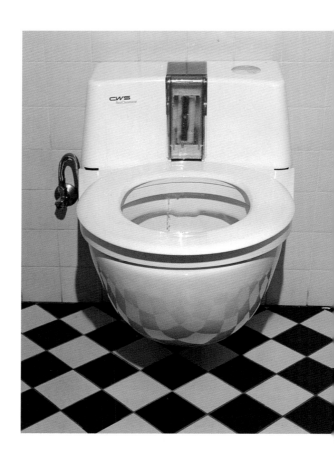

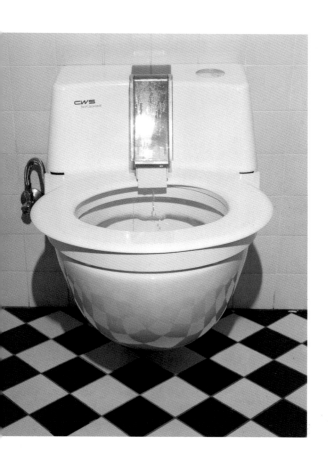

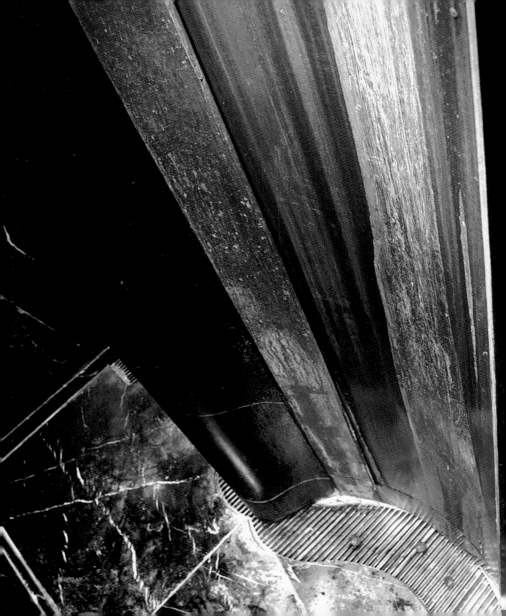

Majestic
rue du Magistrat
ussels

this sumptuously
corated bar, a visit to the
mmodities is as luxurious
experience as the rest. The
oduced lighting creates an
nosphere of chic elegance.
e floor-to-ceiling, wall-to-
ll urinal is automatically
tivated when the user steps
to it. A waterfall gushes
wn the marble face until
e user steps back.

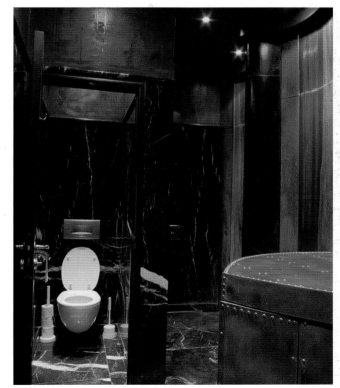

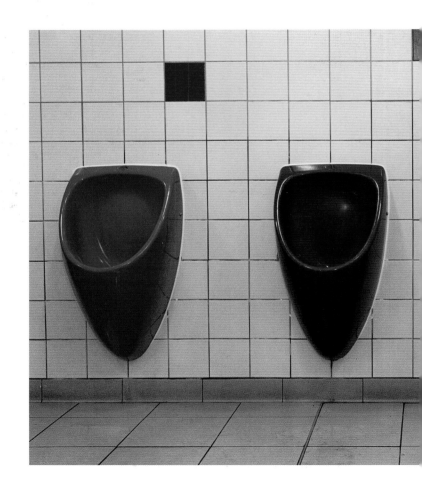

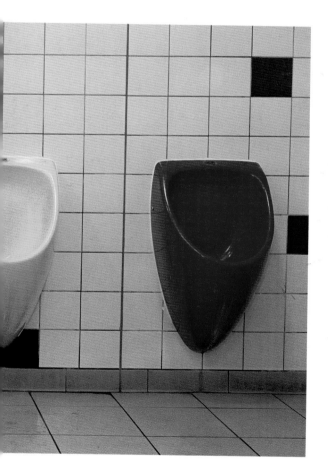

Legoland
Windsor
Berkshire

Even the urinals in Legoland are colourful and clever innovations. Inspired by Lego colours and developed by Falcon Waterfree Technologies, these units contain cutting-edge water conservation technology. They require no water. Instead, a cartridge containing a layer of liquid sealant is placed in the bottom. The sealant is lighter than water, so liquid is immediately trapped beneath and released into the drain, eliminating the need to flush. This efficient system saves an average of 150,000 litres (40,000 gallons) of water per urinal per year.

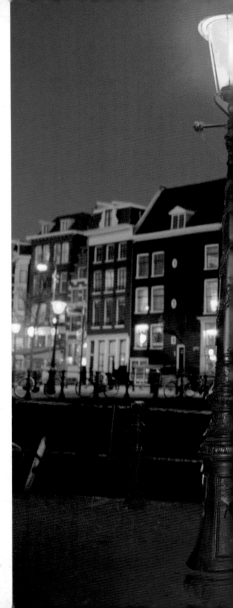

The Netherlands

**Singel Canal and
Brouwersgracht
Centrum
Amsterdam**

Pisbak or *pissijn* is how the
Dutch refer to their public
urinals. These shell-shaped
metal urinals can be found
in several places along the
canals of Amsterdam. Despite
the grid of holes around the
urinal's exterior, the user can
be clearly seen only up to
his knees.

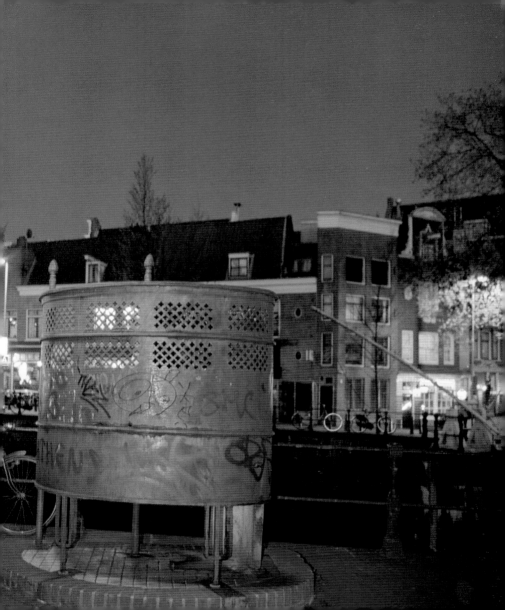

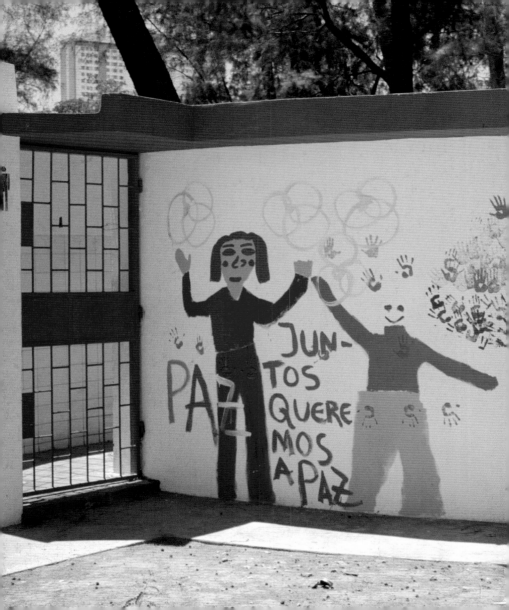

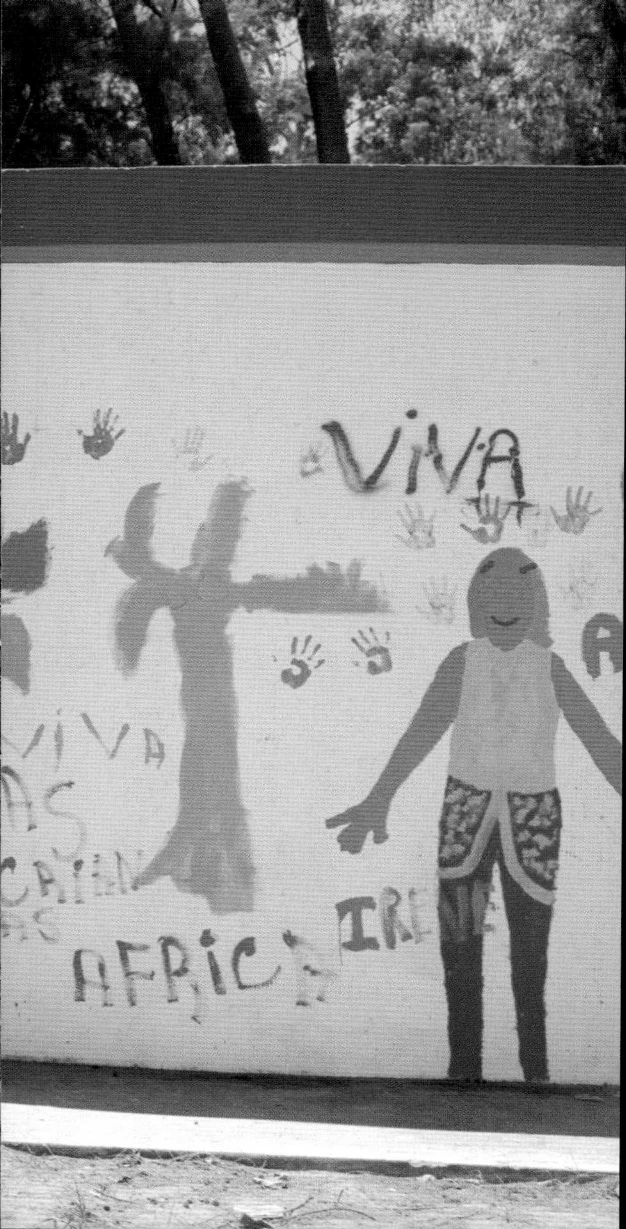

Toilets of Africa

The great continent of Africa is the cradle of humankind and thus also the home of the first person to use the toilet some two million years ago. The term 'toilet' is used loosely in this case, as the act certainly took place in a field or river or behind a bush. Africa is associated with tribal peoples, vast deserts and savannahs teeming with wildlife. It has plenty of these to offer and much more. The toilets throughout Africa reflect not only geographical and cultural variety but also the darker side of economic and social disparity, past and present.

A land rich in countless cultures and languages, Africa changes greatly from one region to the next. Like landscapes, wildlife, dress and customs, different areas also have different toilets. Although squat toilets are common in the North African Arabic countries, they seem to become increasingly rare as one moves south. In the southernmost African countries, even rural family outhouses are generally built for sitting rather than squatting. In this case the pedestal is often made of wood or stone. Like most of the world, the Western-style porcelain facility is common in affluent urban centres.

Outhouses are common on farms and in villages of rural Africa. They are usually constructed of local clay but may also be made of wood or brick. Building materials are even more basic in the poverty-stricken townships and settlements, where anything from sheets of plastic, metal, sticks and dried cornstalks are used. In the southern countries in particular, the door to the outhouse is often hingeless – a brightly painted door simply propped against the entrance is a regular sight.

Africans have adopted a clever way of using the sun's searing heat to ventilate the rural toilets. Brilliant in their simplicity, these outhouses are a runaway success. They are made inexpensively from readily available materials and do not require running water. For durability's sake, there is no door. Instead the structure is spiral-shaped, with the toilet area being the centre of the 'snail shell'. A ventilation pipe runs from the pit below up through the roof. The outer portion of the pipe is heated by the sun, which causes air and therefore odour from the latrine to be sucked up and expelled from the top of the pipe. The toilet is either a simple hole in the floor or

edestal type, depending on
cal preference.

ysterious, fascinating and
mplex, Africa preserves
cient beliefs while working
rd to improve current
ing conditions. Disease,
riculture, irrigation,
nitation, health and
ucation are a few of the
ues being tackled with
rying degrees of success
ross the continent today.
they do elsewhere on
e planet, the local toilets
veal customs, lifestyles
d even history specific to
rticular locations. Intrepid
venturers straying from
e beaten path experience
e birthplace of humanity
sthand. They also gain a
eper understanding of
rican culture by way of
artheid toilets, toilets
me to fur seals, barbed
re toilets and even entire
lds of toilets.

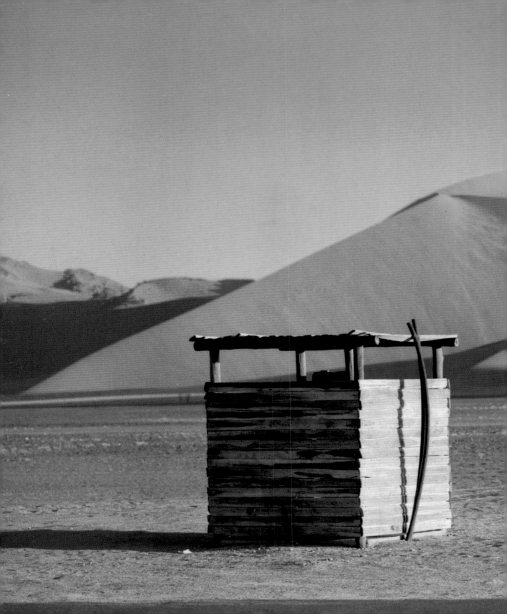

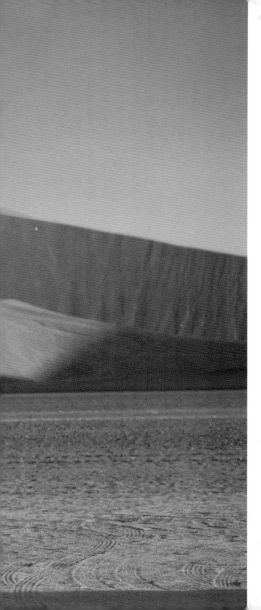

**Dune 45
Sossusvlei
Namib Naukluft Park**

Shadowed by the world's
highest sand dunes, this
simple wooden outhouse
has a breathtaking backdrop.
The red dunes of the Namib
Desert provide a stunning
display as light, colour and
shadow change by the
minute. This solitary toilet
bears witness to the constant
movement of endless skies
and shifting sands.

135

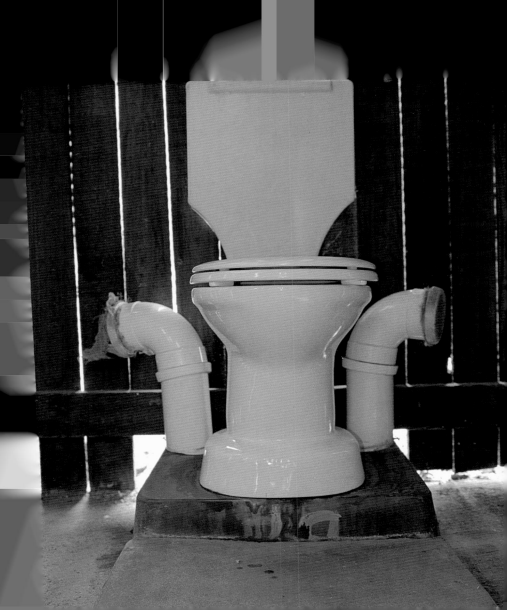

rpen Dam Lookout
ruger National Park
lpumalanga

ocated in South Africa's most
mous game park, these
uthouses are completely
dour-free. This is thanks to
ne external turbines, which
xtract the air. The ventilation
pe heats up in the sun,
ausing an upward draught
om the latrine pit below the
toilet. Oddly enough, the two
pipes protruding from the
toilet itself go nowhere. The
grunting heard from these
toilets actually comes from
the nearby resident hippos.
When this photo was taken,
a bull elephant was bathing
in the nearby river while a
crocodile basked in the sun.

*A herd of elephants stops
traffic en route to the toilets.*

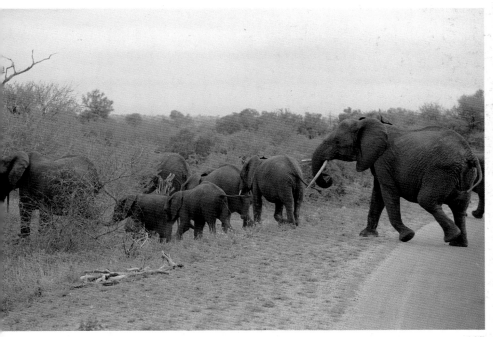

Kuiseb Campsite
Kuiseb Canyon
Erongo

Located on the Tropic of Capricorn, this toilet is built on the bank of the dried-up Swakop River. The mound on which it is perched is made of stones gathered from the riverbed. The Swakop River got its name from the Nama word *tsoakhaub* which means, in polite terms, excrement. The river was so named because of the filthy mass of mud and debris it spews into the clear Atlantic on the rare occasions that it floods. On 22 December, the sun's rays beat down vertically on the Tropic of Capricorn. With temperatures reaching well over 40°C (104°F), beware of the effect of a black plastic toilet seat on a bare bottom.

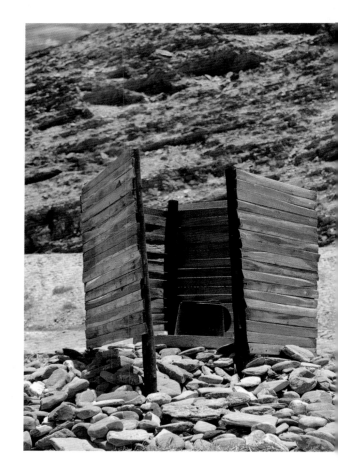

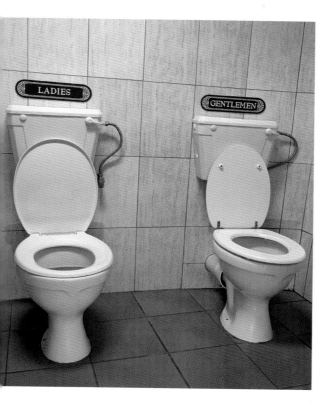

iamond Diggers Lodge
i Doris Street
ensington
Mannesburg
auteng

stead of a cubicle, the term
r a typical single-toilet stall,
is is a 'tubicle'. The two
ilets in the same stall are
e result of a plumber's error

during construction. He
placed the evacuation pipes
too close together, making
the placement of two
standard-size doors
impossible. The owners of this
deluxe backpackers' lodge
had the toilets installed
anyway, creating a unique
his-and-hers tubicle.

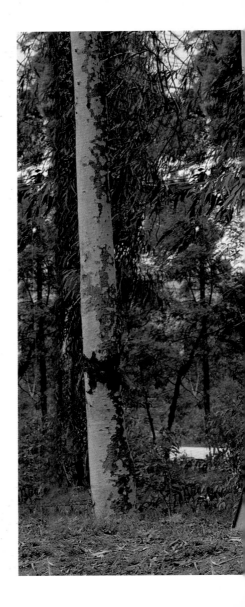

Swaziland

The General Store
Mlilwane Road
Emakhuzweni
Lobamba

Nestled in a gum-tree grove,
this toilet is located behind
the village general store.
During the monsoons, the
red clay sand splashes up,
creating a rich two-tone
exterior. The panel propped
against the entrance is
typical of outhouse doors
throughout southern Africa.

140

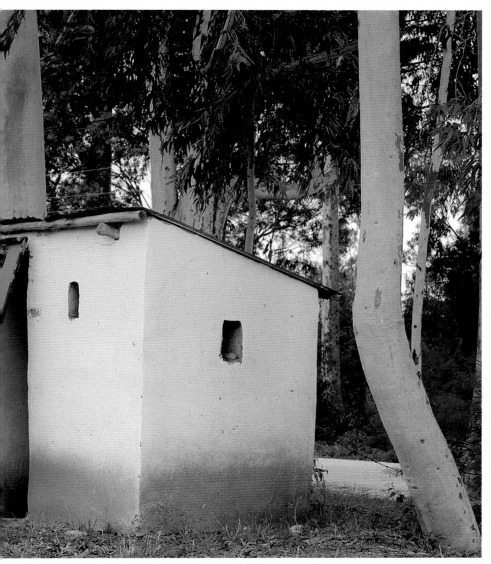

Esitjeni Primary School
Emakhuzweni
Lobamba

Although Swaziland is catching up with modern times, the facilities of village schools remain rustic. These primary school toilets are on the edge of the playground. This is the row of boys' toilets. Inside there are merely holes in a stone floor. In a separate building the girls' facilities are sit-down toilets, some round, others square or triangular – geometric shapes to inspire the developing mind. Stacks of old course material beside each toilet serve as toilet paper.

The girls' toilets – this one a square shape – are carved from local stone.

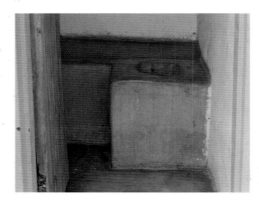

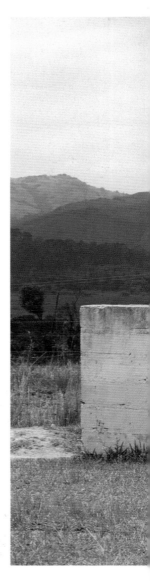

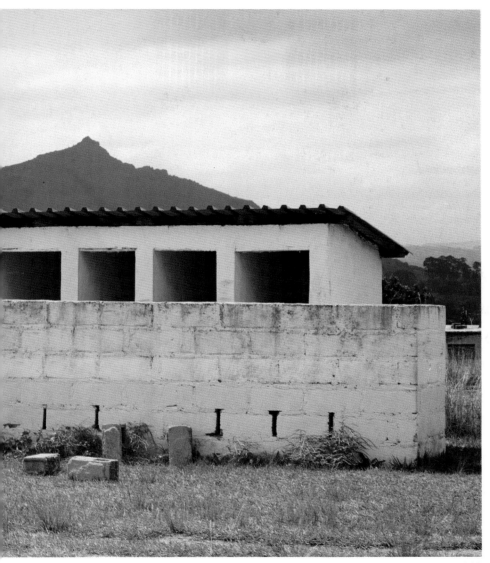

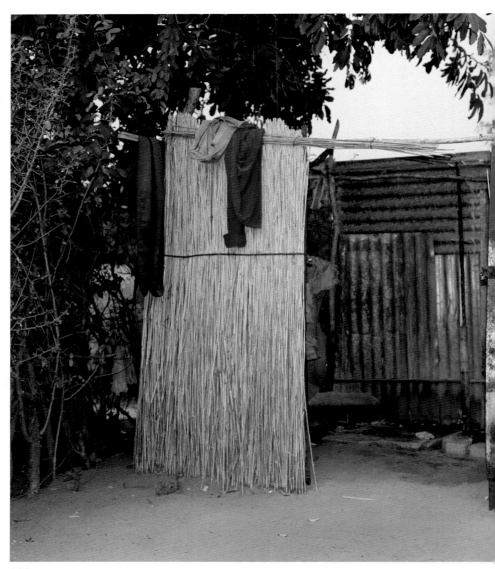

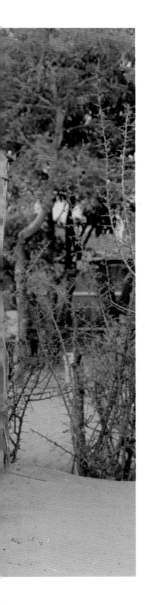

Bairro de Maxaquene 'B' Maputo

This is a private family toilet in a *bairro*, Portuguese for township. During the civil war in Mozambique (which ended in 1992), there was a mass migration of rural populations into the cities for safety reasons. This resulted in the creation of ghettos, where many communities remain as they lack the means to move elsewhere. The threat of one million unexploded landmines scattered in Mozambique's countryside makes it unsafe for families to return to their homelands. Living conditions are rudimentary, with dirt floors and no running water or electricity.

Mozambique

The Old Market
Newtown
Johannesburg
Gauteng

Johannesburg's first public toilet was built in 1911 next to the public market. Despite its charm, this Edwardian building is a harsh reminder of South Africa's turbulent past. The word 'Gentlemen', written in English above the entrance, implies that the toilet was for white men only.

(There were no public toilets for white women in those days as it was considered improper for a lady to relieve herself outside the home.) The luxurious gentlemen's toilet had running water and private cubicles. A servant stood on a podium in the centre of the room, distributing towels and shining the gentlemen's shoes.

Although apartheid did not become official policy until 1948, racial segregation was widespread long before then. Behind the elegant gentlemen's facilities were two discreet side entrances for the black people. The contrast between the toilet for whites and blacks was striking. The black men's urinal was a rudimentary stone trough along the wall and their toilets were keyhole-shaped holes in the stone floor.

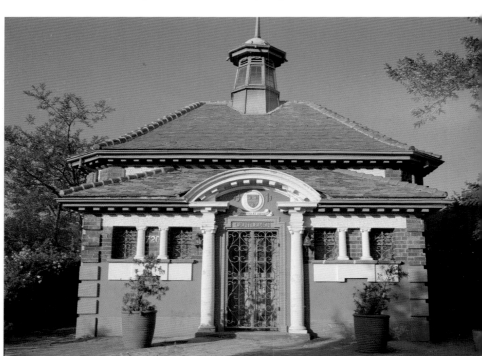

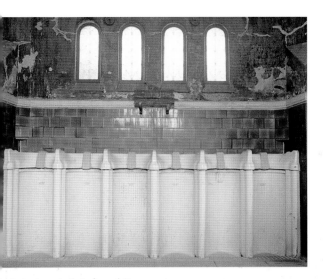

...e luxurious toilets for white men.

...lets for the black people at the back of the building.

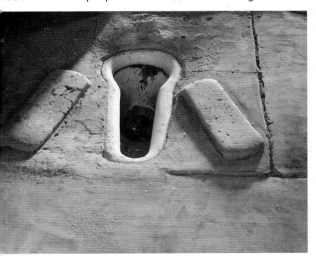

**Parque do Ginasio de Maputo
Avenida 25 de Setembro
Maputo**

Situated in central Maputo, this park is a leafy green oa where the cool shade of an ancient tree provides shelte from the blistering midday sun. This public toilet reflec the typical colourful style o local Mozambican artists. The round structure is decorated with lively image punctuated with phrases in the national language of Portuguese.

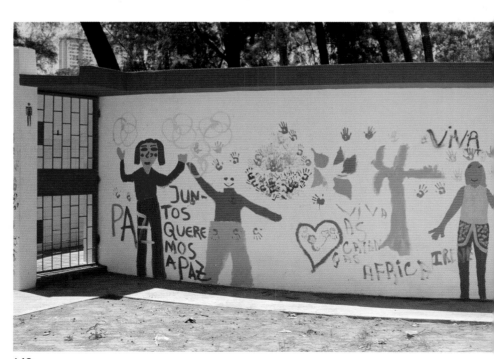

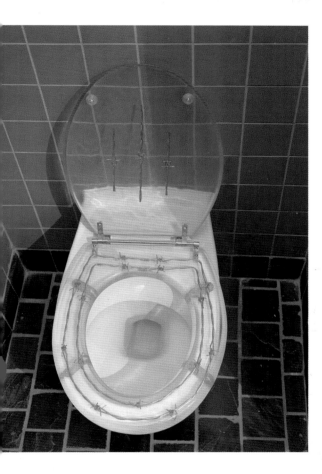

**Underdog Productions
4 The High Street
Melrose Arch
Johannesburg
Gauteng**

To anyone who has ever been to Johannesburg, this toilet seat serves as a stark reminder of the residential neighbourhoods. For security reasons, each property is completely walled in and coils of barbed wire top each wall. Although this toilet appears disturbingly uncomfortable, there is no need to fear the shredding of buttocks. The barbed wire is safely embedded in the clear resin toilet seat.

149

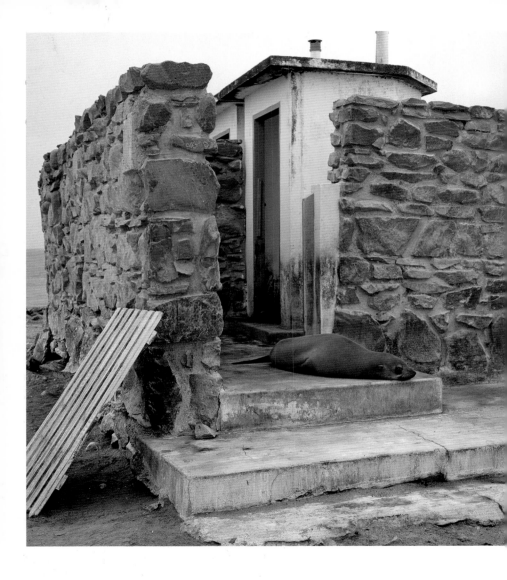

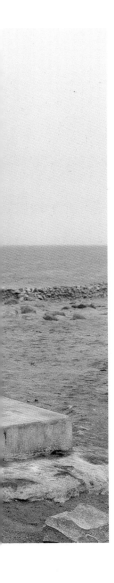

Cape Fur Seal Colony
Cape Cross
Skeleton Coast
Erongo

Imagine tens of thousands of voices repeating "Heeey!" in different pitches, at different intervals and all at the same time. Then you will get an idea as to the cacophony of the Cape Cross fur seal colony. The noise is nothing compared to the stench. One hundred thousand fish-eaters with foul breath flounder over flattened, rotting seal pups. Many visitors pause to vomit as they leave the odourless haven of their vehicles. The family that colonized these toilets are the clever ones. They are the only seals with a bit of elbow room, and the toilets smell much better than the colony.

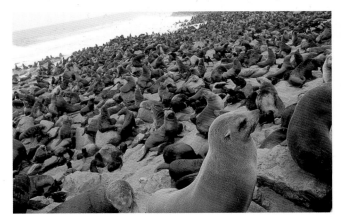

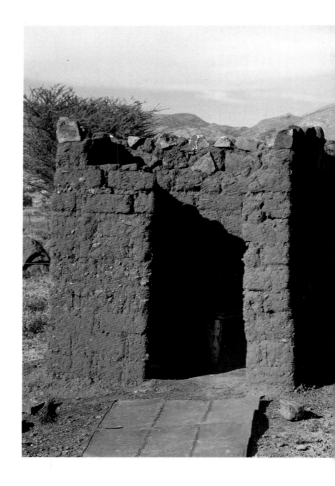

Closer Settlement
Leboeng
Limpopo

Home-made bricks are used to build private toilets in this township. The abundant local red clay is poured into moulds and left to dry in the sun. The toilet itself consists of two wooden planks across a few stones. The hole underneath is generally 12 metres (40 ft) deep and therefore rarely fills to the brim. Should this happen, the hole is covered over and a new one is dug elsewhere on the property. The original bricks are often displaced to build the new toilet.

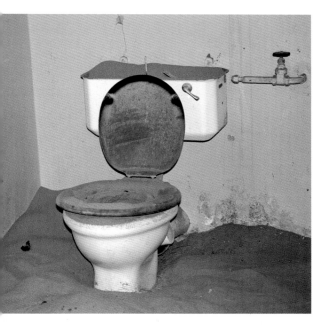

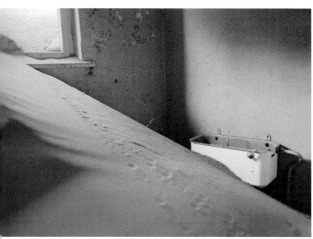

Kolmanskop Ghost Town
14 km (9 miles) east
of Lüderitz
Karas

Following the discovery of diamonds in Namibia in the early 1900s, Kolmanskop flourished as a German colonial mining town. Although located in the middle of the barren desert, the town boasted luxuries such as an ice machine, a theatre, a casino and a bowling alley. Diamond prices plummeted after World War II, at the same time that richer diamond fields were discovered further south. By 1956 Kolmanskop had become a ghost town, deserted and left alone to be reclaimed by the sand dunes.

The dunes are encroaching on the ghost town's hospital.

South Africa

**Closer Settlement
Leboeng
Limpopo**

The South African government's Reconstruction and Development Program is responsible for this impressive field of hundreds of toilets. With the intention of providing low-cost housing, the government first built a toilet to stake each lot. Many years later, both the people and the toilets are still waiting for their houses.

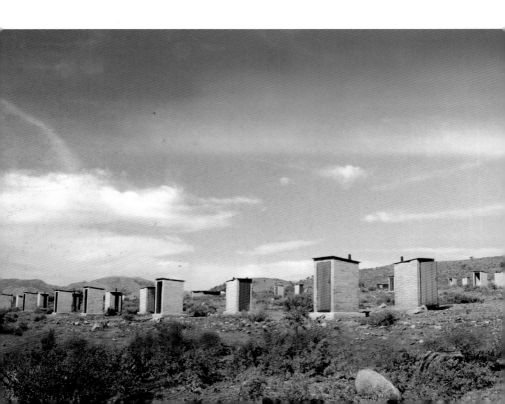

Mlilwane Wildlife Reserve
Lobamba

The thatched roof of this public toilet is the traditional Swazi 'beehive' construction, made by thatching grass under a covering of rope lattice. This toilet is found at the entrance to Swaziland's oldest-established game reserve and local wildlife is commonly seen grazing nearby. When a visitor enters the park, crocodiles, bontebok, zebras, springbok and impala raise their heads in wary acknowledgement.

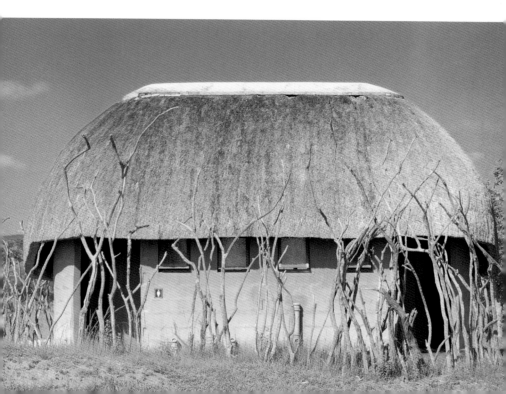

**Kilimanjaro Nightclub
17 The High Street
Melrose Arch
Johannesburg
Gauteng**

The toilets in this popular nightclub glow with the eerie light of the back-lit glass walls on which these steel urinals are mounted. The modern design and mellow light inside these washrooms provide a relaxing haven from the throbbing chaos outside.

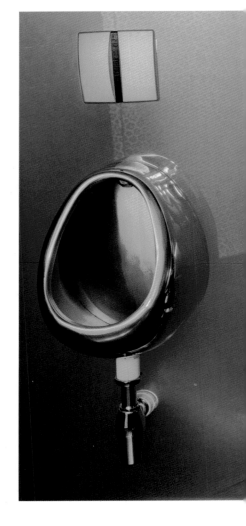

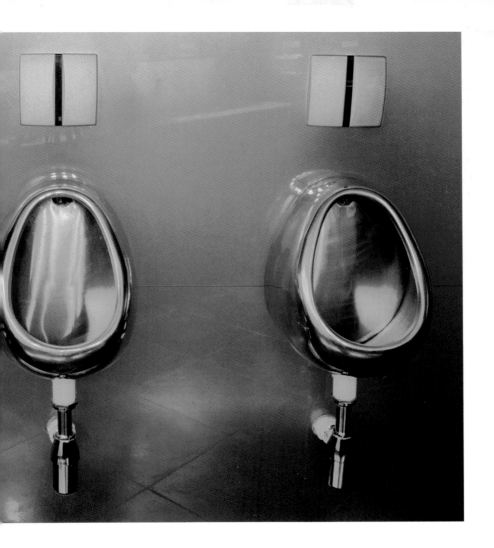

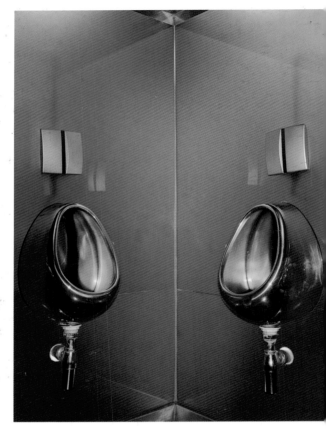

The Kilimanjaro Nightclub toilet collection.

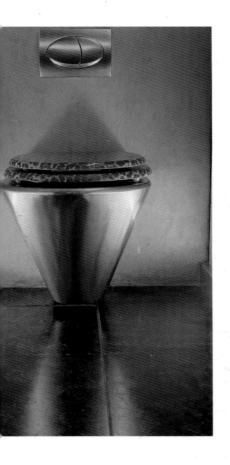
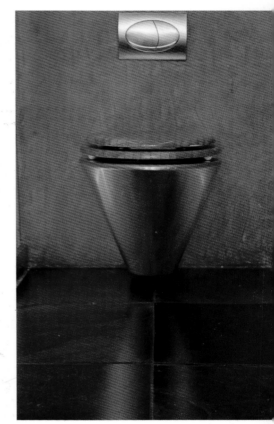

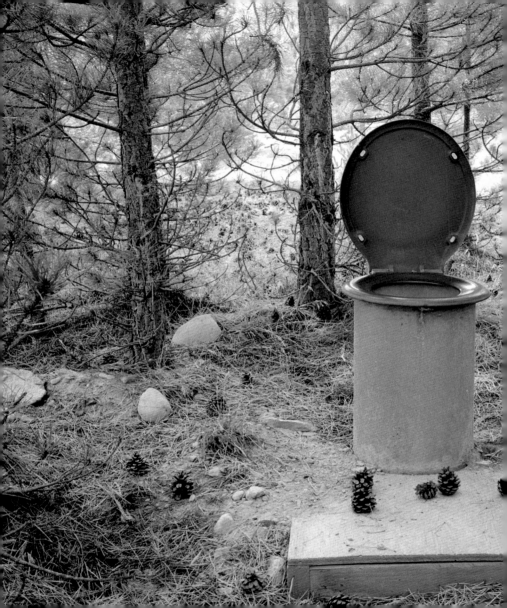

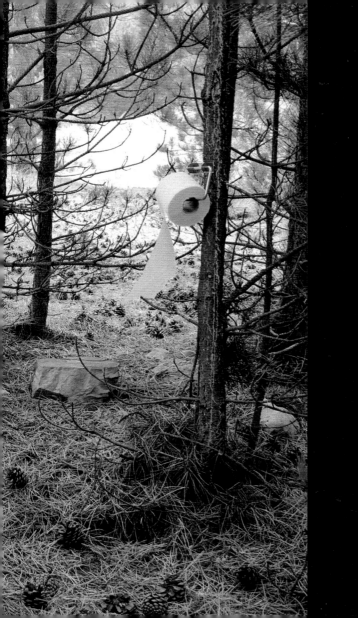

In local loo lingo, when your 'mate goes to the dunny', your friend is going to the toilet, and the outhouse is the 'longdrop'. As the driest continent on earth, excluding Antarctica, Australia has long equipped its toilets with water-saving devices. The dual-flush toilet is installed systematically throughout Australia and New Zealand. These toilets, incorporating two flush buttons, allow the user to select a standard flush or water-saving half-flush according to need. The determining factors for using big flush or little flush are self-evident.

A land rich in iron ore makes steel a plentiful commodity. Dunnies and longdrops are often made of steel, as is the iconic men's toilet down under: the trough urinal. Massive communal steel urinals are found in all sorts of establishments throughout the land. Usually the length of the entire wall, they are great slabs of metal with a drain running along the floor. They offer no privacy from fellow patrons, but Aussie and Kiwi men use them unabashedly from their earliest childhood.

Cities in Australia and New Zealand are modern and lack none of the amenities of other urban centres worldwide. Outside the citi most of the land is sparsely populated and certain rura areas in both countries still lack plumbing. There are many citizens whose only facility is a shack situated a short distance from the house. In the Australian outback in particular, everyone has a tale to tell of an encounter with a loca creepy-crawly in the dunny Stories of poisonous spider and snakes, bats, wombats and even crocodiles abound as frightening as they are humorous. It is easy to imagine why trying to shoo snake in the pit of a longdr is such a messy affair.

An introduction to the toilets of Oceania would be incomplete without commenting on the widespread rumour that water in the toilet swirls in the opposite direction dow under. First, the water in these toilets usually doesn' swirl at all – the water is expelled in one great pressurized jet rather than swirling around in the bow Second, toilet water in the southern hemisphere does not swirl the other way. Contrary to popular belief, the direction in which wate drains from sinks and toilet depends purely on such

hnicalities as bowl shape
d piping. Only in very large
dies of water is the Coriolis
ect, as it is known,
ceptible. Even a toilet
eral kilometres in diameter
uld be too small to exhibit
counter-clockwise flow.

stralia and New Zealand
countries of ecologically
ndly toilets, steel
traptions and longdrops.
stralia in particular has its
re of dunny-related quirks.
Australian government
invested a great deal of
e and money to compile
interactive website listing
ry single one of the
usands of public toilets
oughout the country.
ssies now have the
celess option of pre-
nning toilet stops along
given route and can even
n up for the quarterly
tional Public Toilet Map
vsletter. The following is
a fact of Australian
nnies: when manufacturers
t toilet capacity according
pecifications per country,
y flush varying sizes of
thetic sausages in
ndoms down a set of test
lets. All but the Australian
t: their specifications call
a condom stuffed with
f balls. To complete this
lection, the land boasts
lets with stick bugs, self-
aning public toilets, toilets

overrun by sheep, collapsible
toilets, loos with views, and
even a toilet that has torn
apart an entire town.

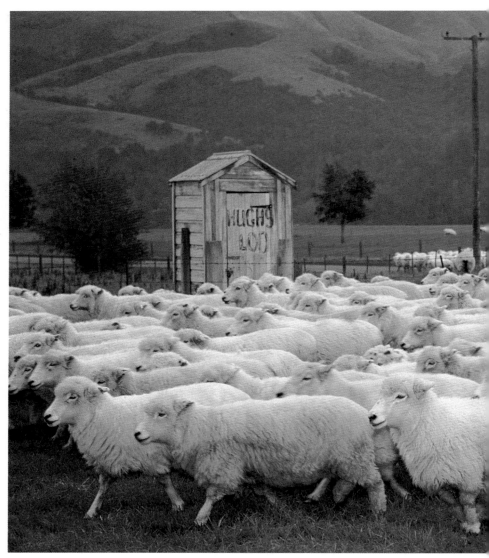

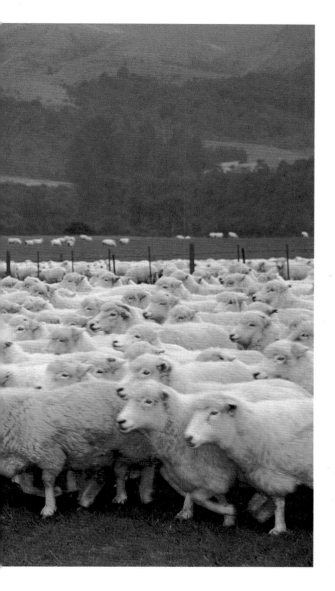

Woodbury Road
Geraldine
South Canterbury

In a country where sheep outnumber people ten to one, visitors to the Canterbury countryside must have no qualms whatsoever about its woolly inhabitants. Thousands roam the vast pastures where this loo stands, and trespassers may find themselves in a sea of stampeding sheep. Squeamish city folk may wish to imagine themselves amid as many cuts of prime New Zealand lamb. Unfortunately, the sheep have no consideration for the patrons of Hugh's loo: tread gingerly on the way for the sake of your footwear.

Gillies Street
Kawakawa
Bay of Islands

The world-renowned Austrian artist and architect Friedensreich Hundertwasser (1928–2000) designed and oversaw the construction of these delightfully eccentric public toilets, situated on the main street of this small town. The toilets attract busloads of curious visitors. Perhaps these are the only toilets that are a tourist attraction not so much for their obvious purpose as for their unique design. Congruity is forgotten here as colourful curves meet unlikely combinations of tiles of all dimensions. The toilets are lit naturally through an odd array of coloured bottles cemented into the wall. The public toilets that put Kawakawa on the map were Hundertwasser's final creation.

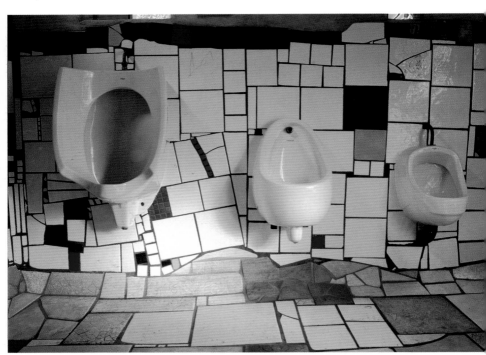

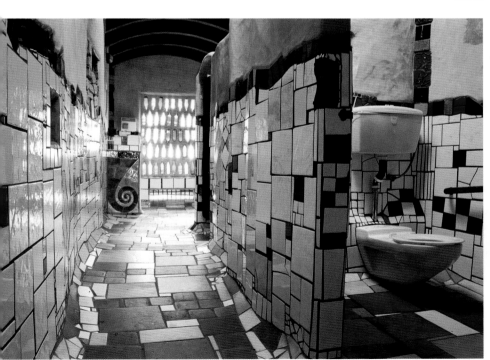

Australia

**Silver City Highway
between Broken Hill and
the Coomba Roadhouse
New South Wales**

Down under, an outhouse is
referred to as a 'longdrop'
and a toilet as a 'dunny'. Why
a farmer felt the need to
erect a longdrop in a paddock
on a remote outback farm is
a mystery. The only ones to
seek privacy from for miles
around out here are the
horses and the kangaroos.
This oddly placed longdrop
was made using sheets of
corrugated steel.

168

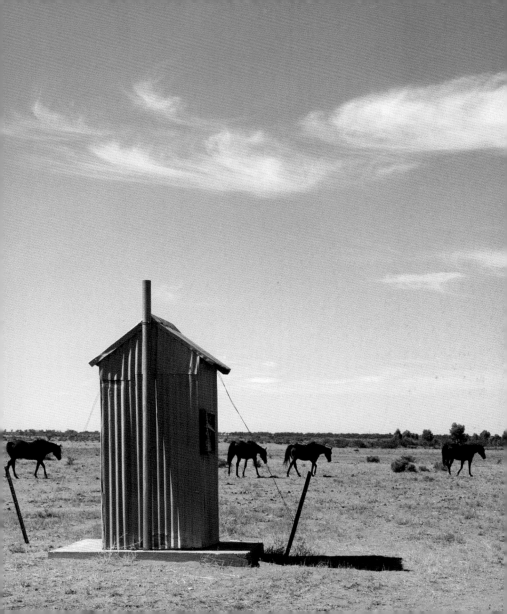

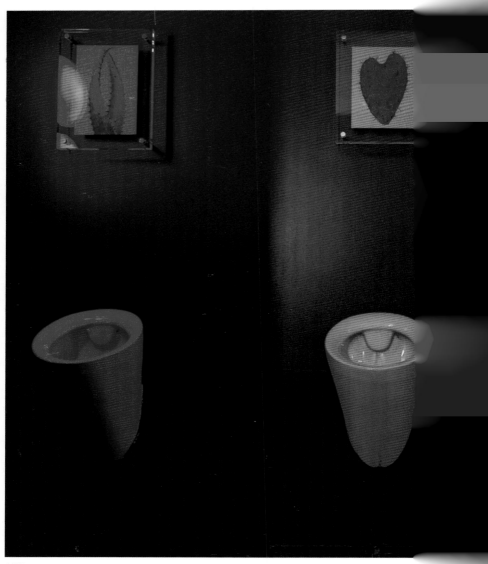

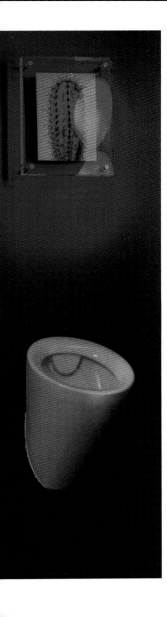

W Hotel
6 Cowper Wharf Road
Wooloomooloo
Sydney
New South Wales

In the early twentieth century, Finger Wharf was lined with busy shipping warehouses, which declined into an unfortunate state of disrepair in the 1960s and 1970s. They have recently been transformed into prime Sydney real estate. The shells of the warehouses have been preserved and inside are spacious lofts. The interior decoration and design of this building have been meticulously executed, right down to the details of the toilets. Lighting is the main accessory in this men's room, where the elegant design of the row of urinals is awash in a mellow red glow.

171

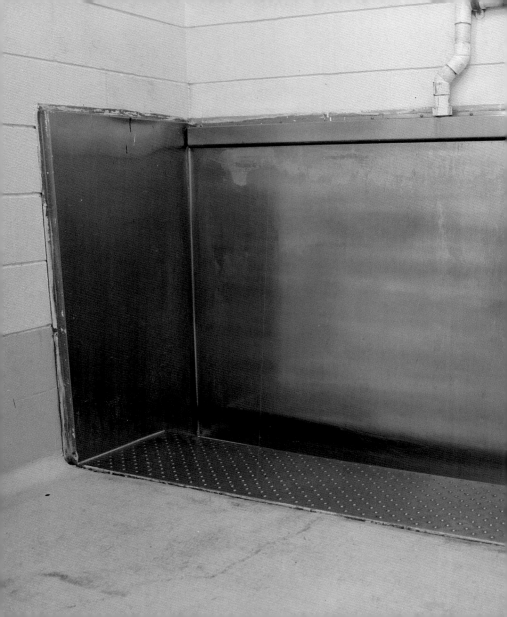

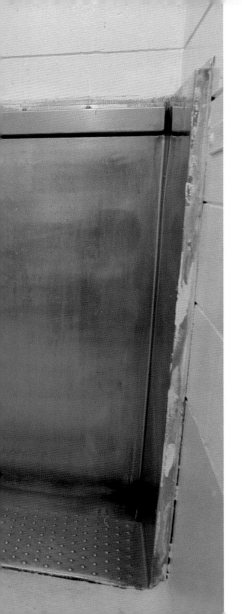

Jellicoe Street
Te Puke
Northland

A town called Te Puke is a must for inclusion in this book. The massive steel wall is the quintessential men's urinal in this part of the world. These great metal urinals can be found everywhere, from dingy bars to fancy restaurants and government buildings. Since they provide no privacy, users must adhere to the unspoken protocol: do not stand too close or too far back, allow fellow users plenty of room and, above all, never glance sideways.

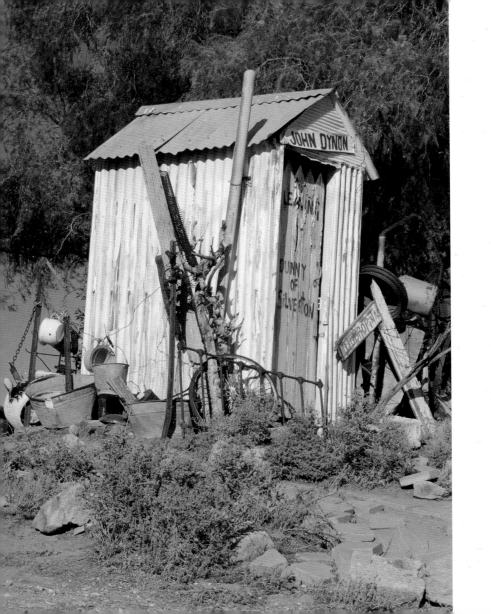

ilverton
New South Wales

A rusty chair frame over a bucket serves as the toilet in the 'Leaning Dunny of Silverton'. This outback outhouse is teetering to one side, though not so much that the beer bottles inside topple off the shelf. Spare buckets and a miscellany of items are piled around outside. The tiny town of Silverton has been the setting of several movies, most famously the *Mad Max* trilogy starring Australia's native son Mel Gibson.

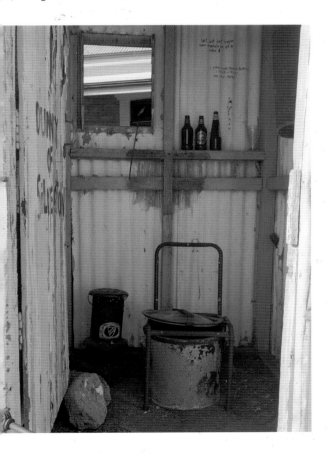

Inside the Leaning Dunny of Silverton.

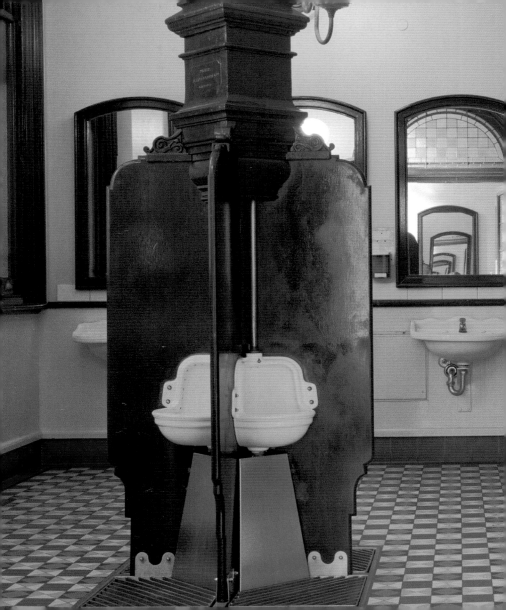

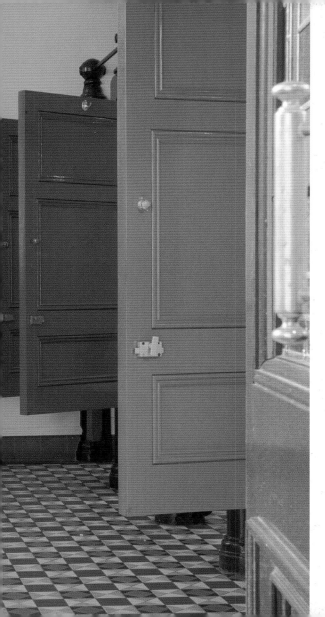

**Queen Victoria Building
George Street
Sydney
New South Wales**

This late Victorian lavatory,
dating from the original
construction of the building
in 1898, features a large cast-
iron urinal column in the
centre of the room. There is
a small white porcelain urinal
in the crux of each partition.
Four men can use it at once,
each with some degree of
privacy. Originally built as
an indoor marketplace,
Sydney's 'QVB' still fulfils
this function today.

177

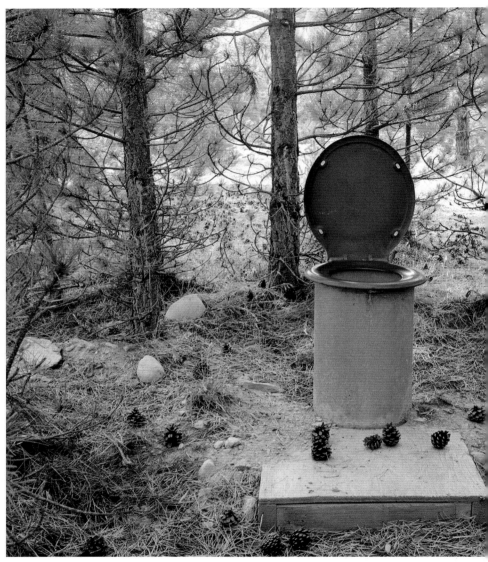

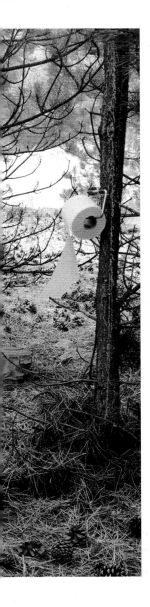

**Mackenzie Alpine
Trekking Company
Mackenzie Basin
Otago**

Clients of this horse-trekking outfit should leave their helmets on when they use this facility. In this peaceful setting the slightest of breezes can bring down a shower of huge pine cones. Once the pine cones have been dodged, many users appreciate the sensation of being at one with nature while seated here.

**Ouyen
Victoria**

The collapsible toilet is a brilliant invention for those travelling to remote corners of the Australian outback. Jimmy's Thunderbox™ folds up neatly into a flat square, light and easy to transport. When far from civilization and the need arises, simply dig a hole to place Jimmy's Thunderbox over. It easily unfolds into a sturdy little toilet. Just like being in the comfort of your own home – well, almost.

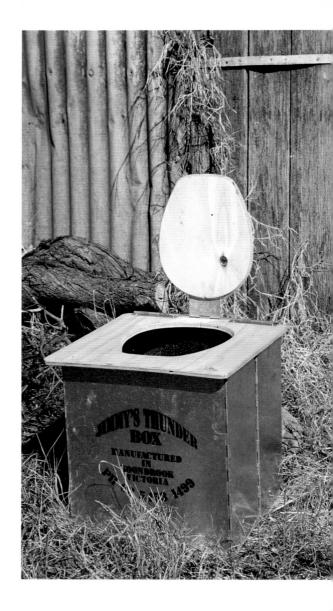

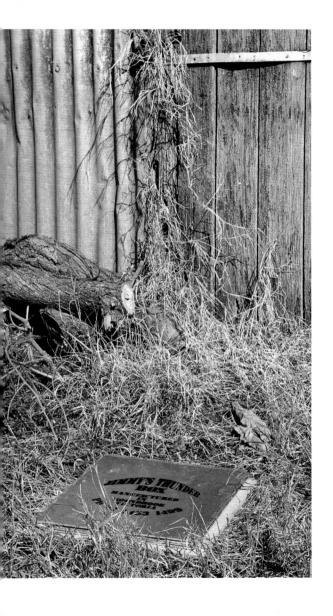

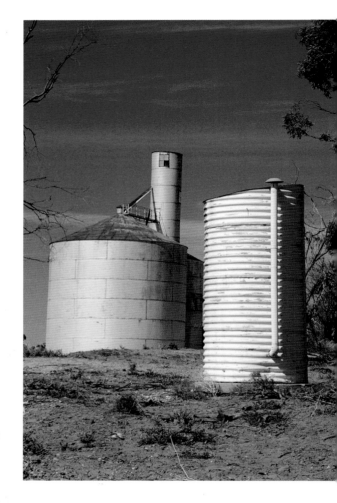

**Calder Highway
between Ouyen and
Mittyack
Victoria**

Echoing the shape of the
silo behind it, this conical
white outhouse is made of
corrugated steel. Silos are
used for mass storage of grain
throughout the year. The
longdrop with its ventilation
pipe is used by farmhands in
the seasons when the silo is
emptied, filled or maintained.
These white structures
contrast sharply with their
vast surroundings of red and
blue hues typical of rural
Australia.

Atrium Cocktail Bar
Collins Tower
Melbourne

From high up on the thirty-fifth floor, users of these urinals can look out over the view of the sprawling city of Melbourne. The floor-to-ceiling window evokes a haunting sense of vertigo that makes anyone with a fear of heights head quickly back to the elevator. Loos with views are found exclusively in men's rooms. Although it may be impractical, wouldn't it be nice to construct a row of cubicles for ladies where toilets were installed backwards? Instead of staring at the back of a door, women too could enjoy the view.

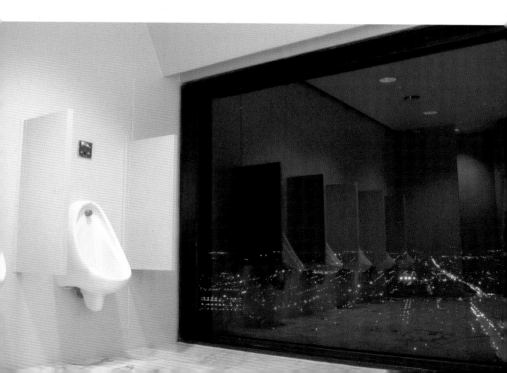

Sign of the Bellbird
Summit Road
near Christchurch

In keeping with New Zealand's eco-friendly image, the Department of Conservation has installed solar-powered toilets along walking trails throughout the country. Running on energy drawn from the solar panel on the side of the structure, a pump pushes the toilet's contents through a filter. The matter then seeps harmlessly into the ground via the toilet's septic system.

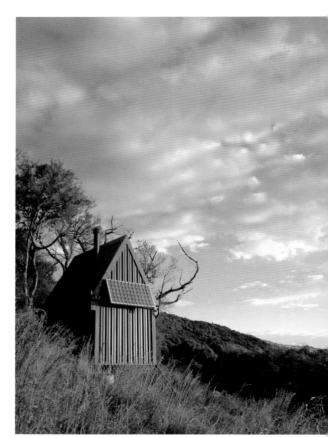

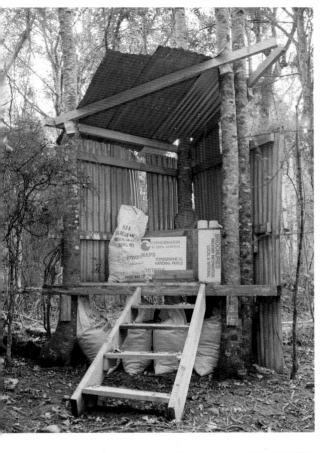

**Outdoor Pursuits Lodge
Peel Forest
South Canterbury**

Nailed to a trio of kehekatea trees, this ecological composting toilet uses no chemicals. Chips of pine bark are regularly thrown down the toilet to the vat below. The compost mixture is removed at regular intervals and used as fertilizer. While using this environmentally friendly toilet, the user can gaze out into the unspoiled native New Zealand forest.

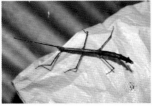

ow often does one use the
ɔilet while in the company
ꞎ a stick insect?

185

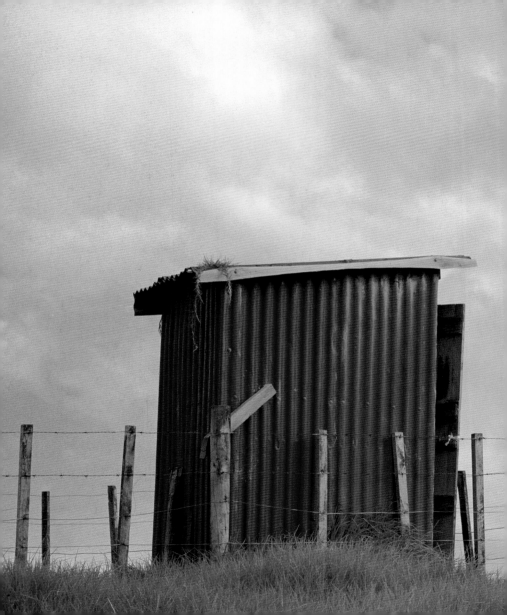

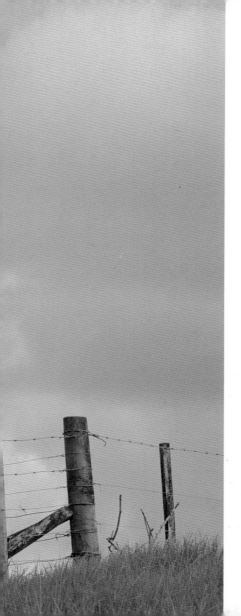

**State Highway 12
Between Omapere and
Waiotemarama
Northland**

Longdrops, or outhouses, are
a common feature of the New
Zealand countryside. In this
case, the drop isn't so long:
rather than being built over a
pit, there is a bucket beneath
the seat. The walls of this
charming longdrop are made
of sheets of corrugated steel
and painted red. Perched on a
grassy hilltop, this rustic shack
is the toilet for the adjacent
Baptist church. It is a nostalgic
reminder of simpler times.

187

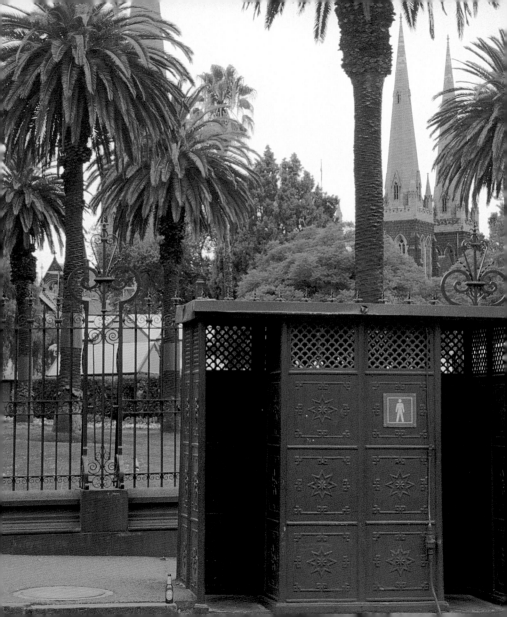

cholson Street and
bert Street
elbourne
ctoria

der the palm trees on a
eet corner in downtown
elbourne stands an old iron
blic toilet. With intricate
otifs cast into the panelling,
een Victorian-era toilets
ch as this are well preserved
d are used regularly
roughout the old sections
the city. At least one
veller made use of the toilet
e previous night, as can be
duced by the beer bottle
the ground beside it.

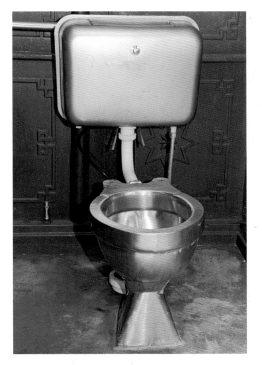

*A gleaming steel toilet inside the cast-iron
building.*

**Aldersyde
Elong Elong
New South Wales**

Ironically, Elong Elong means 'big water hole' to the local Aboriginals, an unusual name for a dry and parched dustbowl. Originally built in the early 1940s, this longdrop was for the seasonally employed sheep shearers. The shearing shed stands behind the toilet. Both buildings were intact until 1996, when a severe tornado ravaged the area. The shed withstood the tornado with minor damage but the longdrop lost its roof and front door. The steel roof of the toilet still lies twisted on the ground.

190

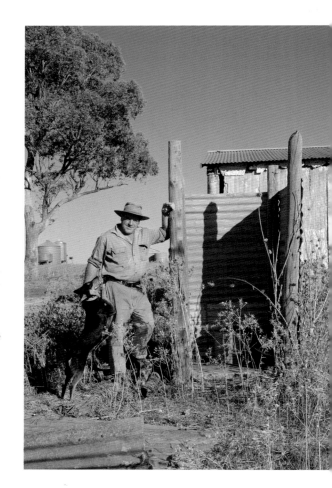

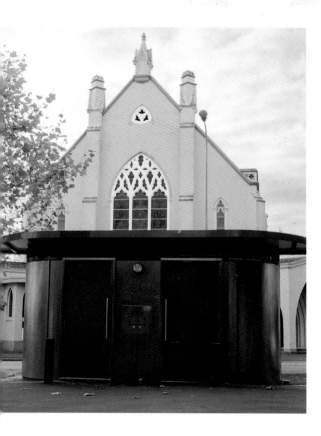

**Creek Lane
off Commercial Road
Helensville
Auckland**

Although the photograph may appear deceptive, this public toilet is not the main floor of a church. Automatic, self-cleaning and vandal-resistant, these sturdy and efficient public toilets have been popping up all over the streets of New Zealand in recent years. The features of this pay toilet operate via sensors, so its functions are all touchless. The user can get toilet paper, flush, and turn on the taps and driers all without touching a thing. The toilet automatically cleans itself from ceiling to floor when unoccupied.

191

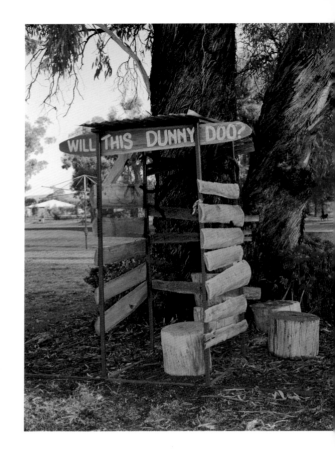

Australia

Dunedoo Caravan Park
Dunedoo
New South Wales

Never before has the solidarity of an entire town been shattered over a toilet. The town's name is pronounced 'dunny-doo', and its 829 inhabitants are bitterly divided over a potential tourist attraction to revive the town: The Big Dunny. Supporters of the construction of the world's biggest outhouse on Dunedoo's main road have been clashing bitterly with opponents since 2000. This dunny, built by a pro-Big Dunny, has been destroyed several times by the anti-Big Dunny camp. At present, the proposal has been rejected by the authorities, but supporters are still rallying passionately to build The Big Dunny of Dunedoo.

An enormous mirrored urinal covers the entire wall of the men's room in this trendy Sydney nightclub. A waterfall is constantly streaming down over the mirror into a small gutter below. When users tire of examining their own reflection, they can watch live scenes from various corners throughout the club on the television screens above.

Australia

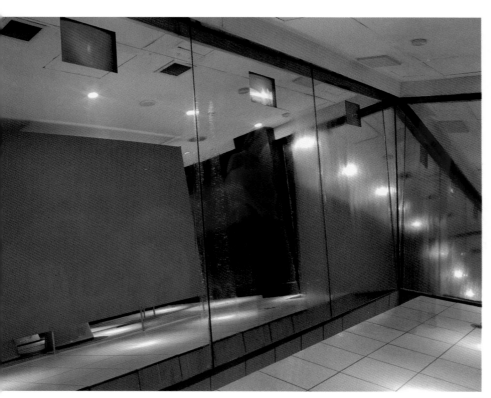

Home Bar
The Promenade
Cockle Bay
Sydney
New South Wales

The idyllic harbour with its boardwalk of trendy restaurants and cafés is not the only view at Darling Harbour. While standing at these urinals, the user has a sweeping view over the crowded bar one floor below. He can study the art of bartending, couple dynamics and the effects of inebriation, all from the privacy of this discreet loo with a view. Although inconspicuous, the steel urinals on their cheery orange wall offer an appealing sight to the toilet-trained eye.

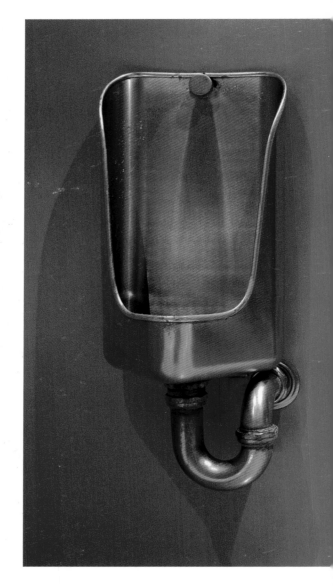

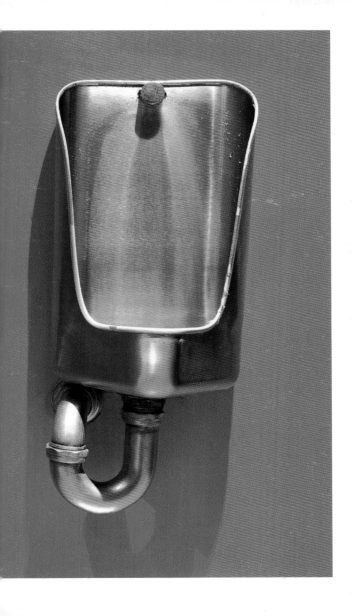

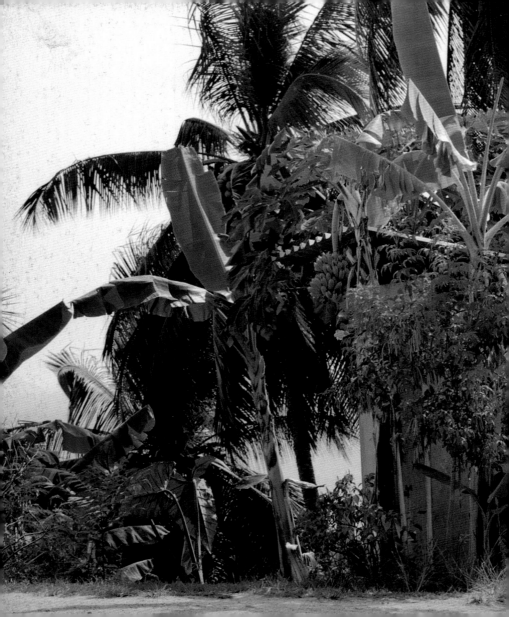

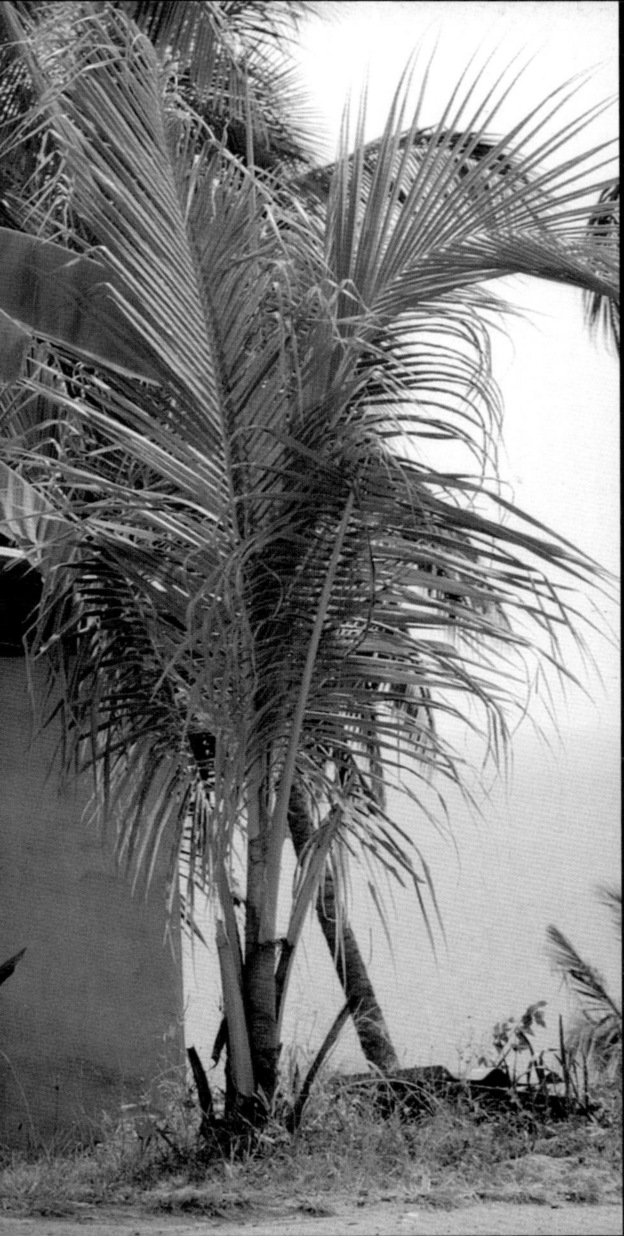

Toilets of Asia

Ancient tradition thrives alongside cutting-edge technology in Asia, giving it that peculiar feel of the merging of old with new. Its geographical immensity and rich history have forged a land of contrasts unlike any other. Asia is comprised of many countries, each very different. It is at once very rich and very poor, moulded by a long and often turbulent past and bold visions of the future. Many aspects of Asian culture are reflected in this kaleidoscopic background, including the toilets. Asia teems with an endless variety, from shallow holes in the dirt to the most outlandish and extravagant toilets in the world.

Most Asians use squat toilets and certain regions have a brand all their own. Thailand has a unique squat, a small raised pedestal with porcelain foot rests on either side of the rim. Japan uses elongated floor squats with a cover on the front end to catch splashing. Public toilets in China are often a slot in the floor above a stream of water. Turkey's loo of choice is the classic squat, a porcelain tray in the floor that incorporates a pair of foot rests and a hole. This design is frequent in India, where a shallow indent in the ground is also used. The side of the road and the train tracks are also choice spots in rural India, but only at dawn and dusk.

Toilet paper habits also diffe across the Asian continent. The Thai use it but do not flush it – paper must be tossed into the bin beside the toilet. In Chinese public toilets, the user pays an attendant for a package of tissue that people in the res of the world would use for their noses. Japan has great heaps of toilet paper: every establishment appears to have mountains of it, which seems redundant with their high-tech wash-and-dry toilets. Turkey and India bot use water and the left hand as a substitute for toilet paper. For obvious reasons it is considered very poor taste to eat or shake hands with the left hand.

Though considered part of Asia, the Indian subcontiner is drastically different from the rest and has its own unique toilet tale. Even in urban centres, fewer than 30% of homes have flush toilets. India's rural inhabitants make up 70% of the entire population and for them the flush toilet percentage plummets to three. Two-thirds of the tota population propagate India' severe sanitation problem by eing forced to practice open efecation. Disease and death e direct consequences of a ck of proper facilities, aiming the lives of a aggering half a million hildren each year. A ground-eaking NGO called the ulabh Sanitation Movement as made great headway in ckling this monumental sue. Sulabh has installed housands of communal and ivate facilities throughout dia. Ten million people in dia now use a Sulabh toilet very day.

stark contrast, the echnological prowess of the nd of the rising sun shines hrough in the facilities of pan. Their wondrous toilets e equipped with heated eats, water jets and blow-ryers. Control panels are ttached to the rim and have selection of spray pressure, ignment and temperature ptions. For bashful users, here is even a button that roduces a loud canned ushing sound. In tourist reas the sign on the door to hese may read "Western", ut they are certainly not estern toilets – good luck nding such a treat in a ublic convenience anywhere the West.

ushing the toilet Asian-style done by a myriad startling or amusing methods. When it doesn't happen automatically via sensors, there is usually a button to be pushed, a handle to be cranked or a plaque to be waved at. Where there is no flush lever, the most common method is to dump a bucket of water down the toilet. For this purpose, washrooms often contain a trough full of water with a small bucket floating in it. A variation is a small tap on the wall to fill the bucket. When toilets don't flush at all, the hole in the ground fills up and the toilet is simply moved to a brand new hole. The great diversity of Asian toilets reaches far beyond the above-mentioned. This continent of delightful extremes is home to cackling-mouth urinals, pig toilets, silk toilet tents, ancient Roman latrines and even toilets made of solid gold.

3D-Gold Store
28 Man Lok Street
Kowloon

All that glisters *is* gold in this awesome bathroom born of a quote from Lenin. A Hong Kong jeweller took the Marxist leader literally when he said that toilets should be made of gold to remind the world of the waste of capitalist warfare. As cited in the *Guinness Book of World Records*, this $3,500,000 washroom is the most expensive on the planet. Fixtures, sinks, taps, toilet brushes and toilet-paper holders are all gold. The gleaming floors are made of petrified wood and inlaid gold, and the ceiling is encrusted with precious gems. The crown jewels of this exquisite lavatory are the two 24-carat solid gold toilets.

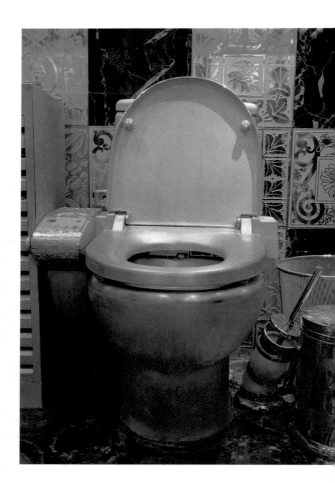

Temporary toilet tents are erected using flashy pink silk reminiscent of the exquisite saris worn by the women of India. These have been set up for Khajuraho's annual celebration of its ancient erotic temples. The two toilet tents emit a distinct smell of curry spices. The men's contains a concrete slab with a small hole, placed over a dugout with two tiny footpads on either side. The women's toilet is nothing more than a shallow indent in the ground.

India

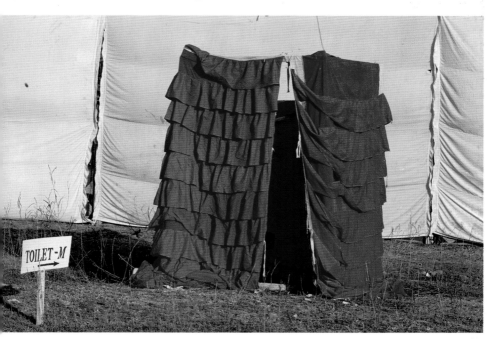

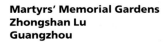

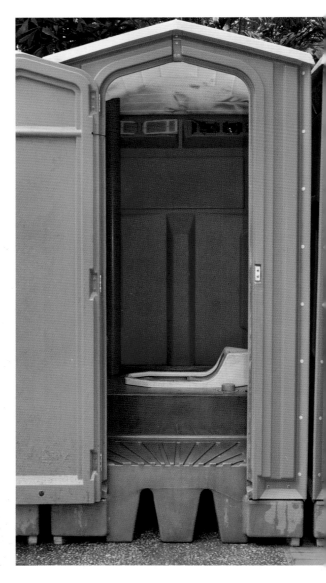

**Martyrs' Memorial Gardens
Zhongshan Lu
Guangzhou**

Most people worldwide are familiar with the porta potty, or the Portaloo. Easy to put up and take down, they are temporarily erected outdoors for such events as fairs or festivals. This row of Chinese portable toilets stands in a public park. Unlike those familiar to Western eyes, these portable toilets feature the typical elliptical Asian squat toilet with a catchment on the front end.

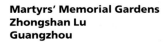

202

Ancient Roman City of Ephesus
Selçuk
İzmir

In Roman times, Ephesus was the mightiest commercial centre in all Asia Minor. Built AD 200, these solid marble communal latrines were situated next to the brothel. They were pay toilets and women were forbidden. They acted as a place of social gathering, where men did their business while discussing current events. Each man had a stick with a wad of fabric bound to one end for cleansing purposes. Their toilet sticks were rinsed in the small gutter that runs along the rows of toilets. This practice is said to be the origin of the expression "getting the shitty end of the stick". Waste from the latrines fell into a pit below and the urine was collected by the tanneries for uric acid.

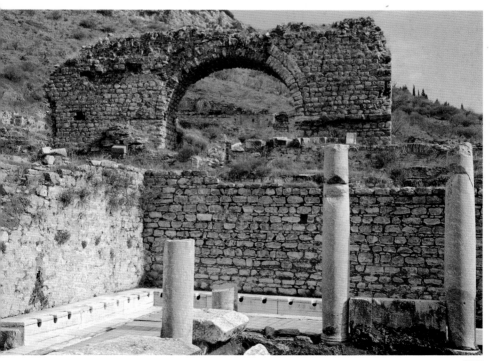

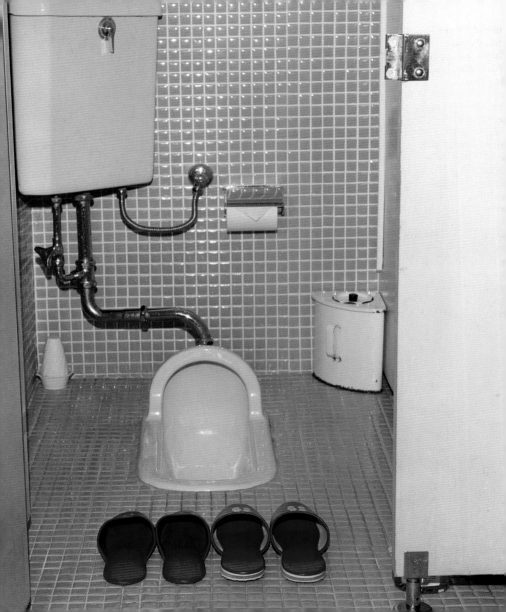

otoshi Ryokan
563 Sano
amanouchimachi
himotakai Gun
agano

ustom in Japanese private
omes decrees that once the
reshold is crossed, guests
ust remove their footwear
nd don one of many pairs of
ppers available at the front
oor. To use the toilet, one
ust then exchange the
ouse slippers for toilet
ppers. Found just inside the
athroom door, these plastic
ppers are easily identified
y the universal man/woman
ilet symbol. When finished
ith the facilities, one must
ange back into household
ppers immediately upon
aving the toilet.

ilet shoes.

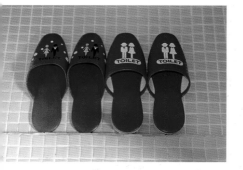
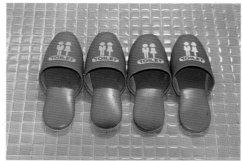

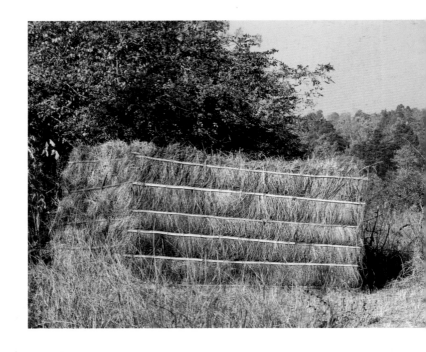

**Panna National Park
Chattarpur
Madhya Pradesh**

Resembling a bale of hay in
a field, this roofless toilet
blends in discreetly with its
natural surroundings. It was
made by thatching the local
grass around a frame of
sticks. Inside, there is simply
a shallow hole dug into the
earth. Stay alert when using
this toilet – the nature reserve
is the feeding ground of
several dozen Indian tigers.

Martyrs' Memorial Gardens
Zhongshan Lu
Guangzhou

The knee-high dividing walls between these women's public toilets provide little privacy. This does not seem to be a major concern; even when doors are present Chinese women often neglect to close them anyway. Behind each of the five half-walls are simple rectangular holes in the floor that share a stream of running water a metre below.

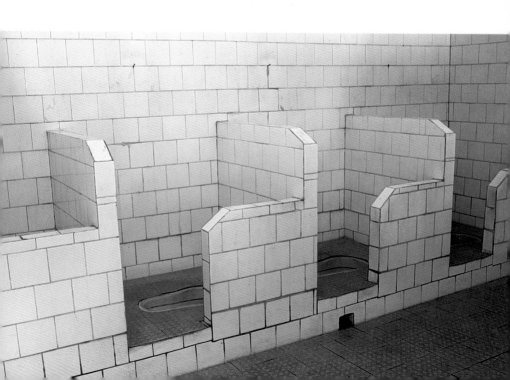

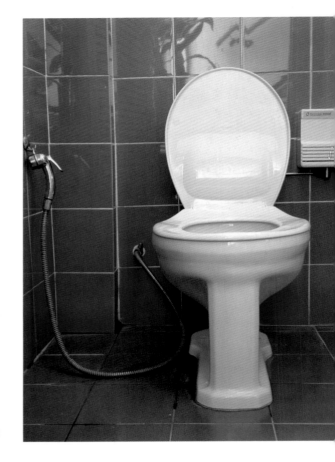

New Road Guest House
1216 Charoenkrung Road
Bangkok

In Thai cities, tourist areas
and wealthier private homes,
toilets generally have modern
plumbing. Wherever the
toilets are plumbed, there is
always a spray gun within
easy reach. The purpose of
the 'bum gun' is obvious. It
diminishes the need for toilet
paper, which wreaks havoc on
fragile Thai plumbing. Paper
is always thrown into a bin,
never flushed.

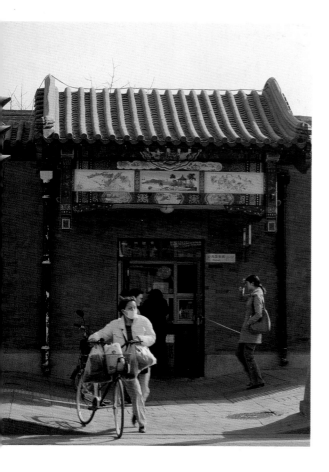

Di'anmen Xidajie
Beijing

The roof of this public toilet along an arterial road in central Beijing is typical of local architecture, complete with a decorated awning. Patrons pay a small fee at the ticket window in exchange for a packet of tissue. Paying to pee in Beijing usually guarantees individual flush squat toilets instead of the more common row of holes sharing a stream of water underneath. Out front, a masked Beijing woman passes by with her bicycle. City-dwelling Chinese often wear face masks as a barrier against pollution and airborne disease, or perhaps the notorious stench of their public toilets.

209

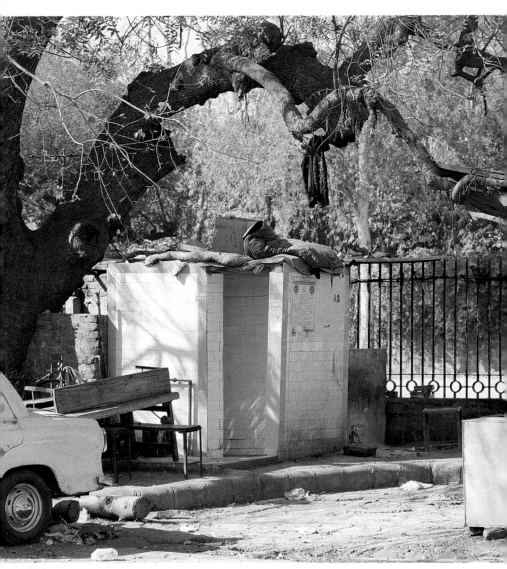

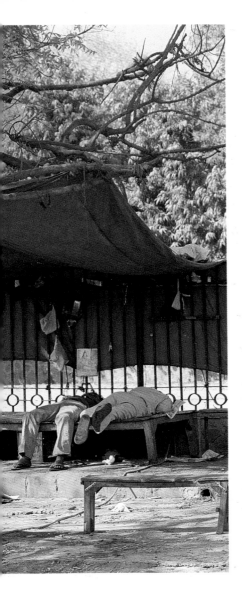

Matya Mahal
Shahjahanabad (Old Delhi)
Delhi

Street-dwellers in India have made a convenient yet somewhat odoriferous home next to this public toilet. Two family members take a nap in the shade to escape the stifling heat of the midday sun. They have stretched blankets across the branches of the tree above, creating a makeshift roof. Their belongings to the left of the toilet include tables and benches. The roof of the toilet is used for storage, where extra blankets are kept in the warmer months.

Ginzadoriguchi
Ginza
Tokyo

No dodgy business will be tolerated in this public toilet a tiny but efficient police station shares the same building. The perfect all-purpose location for those unfortunate enough to have their bag snatched when they really need to go. In the concrete jungle of Tokyo, space is an ongoing problem. This little building makes the most of its space with its dual purpose. Just in front, a policeman surveys the terrain from his bicycle.

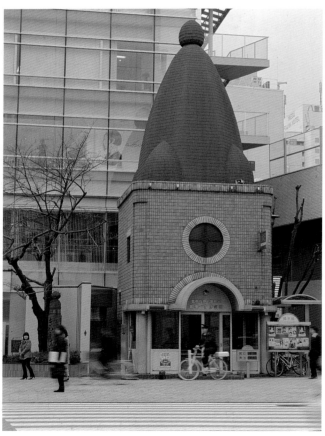

Bhandi Chok
City of Panna
Madhya Pradesh

Cylindrical one-man urinals are a common sight along the streets of Indian towns. They provide the local men with a semi-private place to go, and discourage them from relieving themselves in the open. Although this urinal is intact, they are often found in a very sorry state as they are frequently pillaged for building materials.

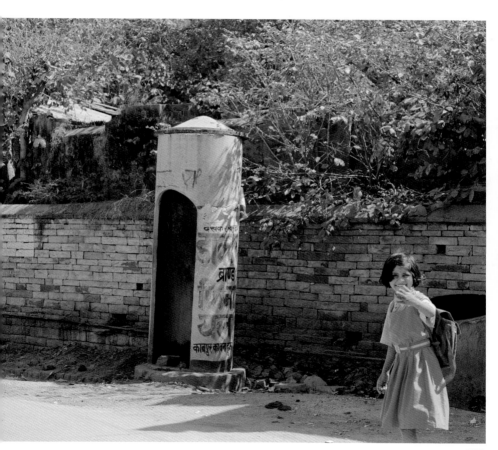

**Toprak Seramik
Cumhuriyet Meydani 12
Alsancak
Izmir**

Children take even more delight than usual in their bodily functions when using these pint-sized kiddie loos. The cute and colourful bear urinal and the kangaroo toilet are specially made for children's bathrooms and are available in five different colours. When installed in private homes, these toilets have to be replaced after a few years since children tend to outgrow their charming potty mates.

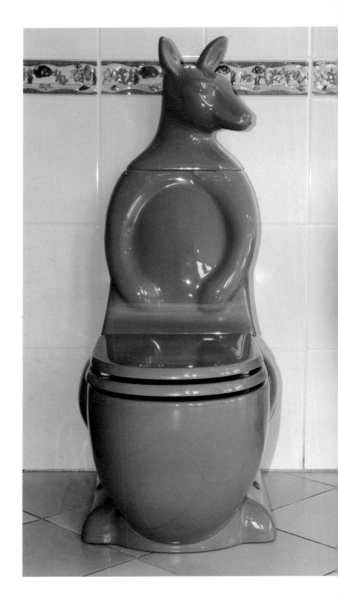

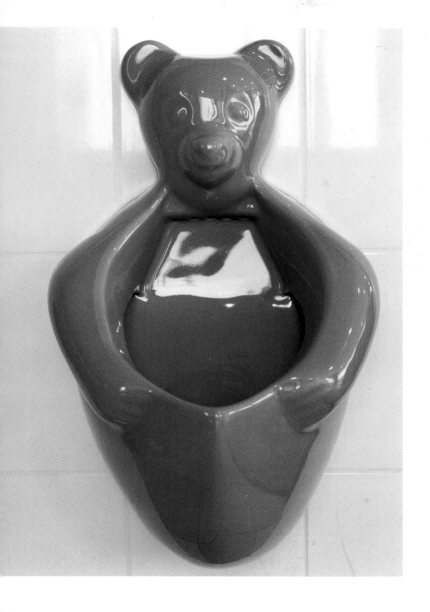

**Mae Klong River
Damnoensaduak**

The sign on this toilet is always cause for mirth with English-speaking visitors to the nearby floating market. "Tolet" was mistakenly painted on it, implying that the left side of the toilet is for rent. Common Thai facilities are found inside, consisting of white porcelain floor-squat toilets. As usual in this country, there is the ever-present bucket and concrete trough filled with water to flush the toilet after use.

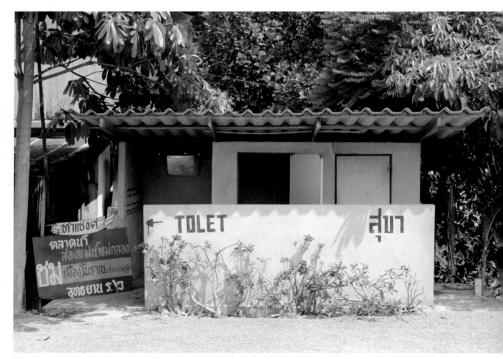

River Kwai
Kanchanaburi

Made of white corrugated steel, this old double outhouse is of the squat variety. Each stall contains a floor-level, one-piece porcelain squat with footprints incorporated on either side. Awkwardly placed behind the toilet is a concrete trough with water and a bucket for flushing.

The infamous bridge over the River Kwai can be seen behind. In 1942–43 Allied prisoners of war and civilian forced labour, under supervision of the Japanese army, constructed the 'Death Railway' joining Thailand and Burma. This route was used to transport supplies to Japanese troops at the Burmese front. In the making of the railway an estimated 96,000 people died, including 18,000 PoWs.

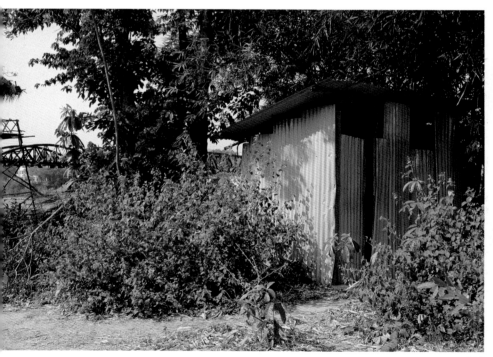

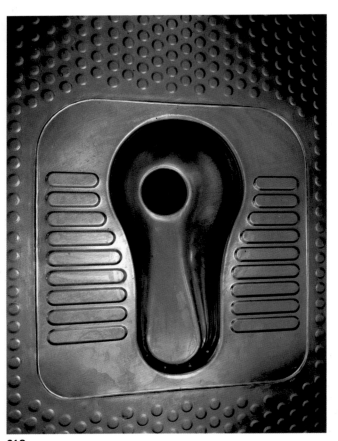

**Soft sleeper car
Guangzhou–Beijing train**

Hold on tight to the handle
on the wall beside this squat
toilet. When flushing, look
down to catch a fleeting
glimpse of the tracks below.
The steel tray is standard
issue on a Chinese train,
regardless of class. All waste
is immediately expelled on to
the tracks, so using the toilet
while stopped at a station is
strictly forbidden. The
advantage of the track flush
is twofold: there are no tank
to empty, and people avoid
the train tracks.

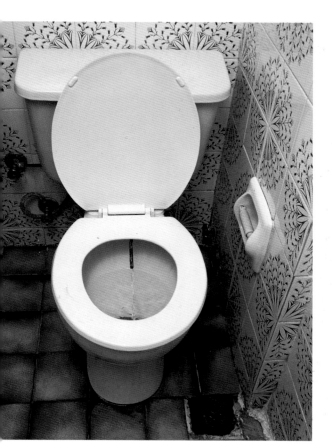

Zeybek Hotel
Fevzipaşa Rulvari 1368
Sokak 6
Basmane
Izmir

Most Turks do not use toilet paper, the Muslim tradition of cleanliness causing them to view it as unhygienic. This merits some consideration. Rather than smearing everything around Western-style, they clean themselves with water. The copper spigot protruding from the back of the toilet serves this purpose. Like a built-in bidet, a steady stream of water is activated by the small red tap on the wall. The user then washes with the left hand. If toilet paper is present, its purpose is for drying only. Fortunately all Turkish toilets have a sink and plenty of soap. It doesn't take a large stretch of the imagination to guess why many sinks also contain urinal pucks.

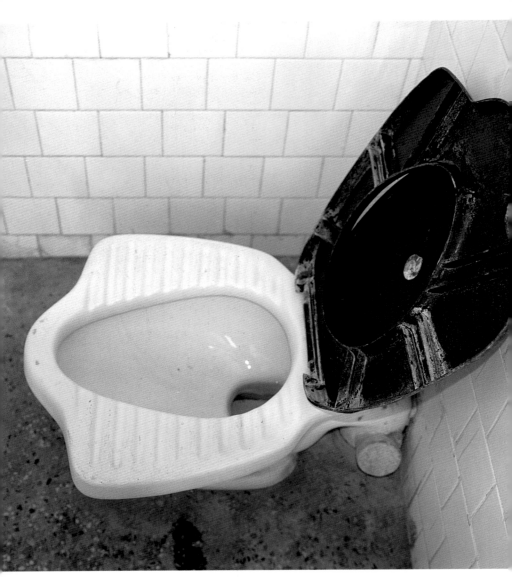

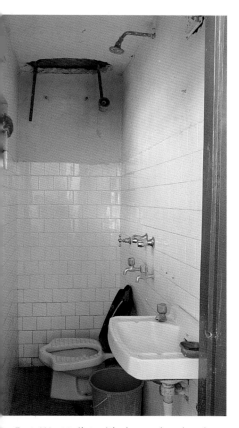

The East–West toilet with shower head and toilet paper.

Cyber Spice Café
Khajuraho
Madhya Pradesh

East meets West with this dual-culture toilet. Like other Asian countries, India took the cue from the Western world and began installing modern toilets. The initial results were disastrous. Rather than sitting on the pot, locals stood on the rim of the bowl or, worse, on the toilet seat, and squatted. As a result, the seats were constantly being broken.

The toilet shown here was engineered in response to this kind of toilet abuse. Users can choose to put down the seat and use it Western style, or flip the lid, stand on the porcelain footprints and squat to their heart's content. The toilet paper roll is ridiculously high – the user has to stand up on the footprints to reach it. Judging by the thick layer of dust, this roll of paper has been untouched for years.

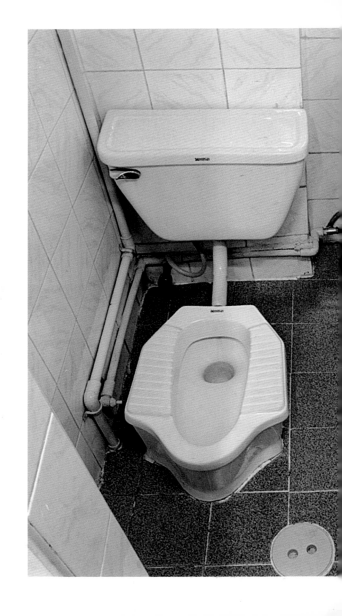

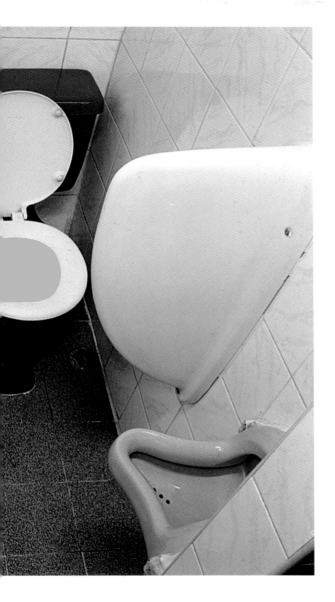

**Toby Jug Pub
185 Silom Road
Patpong
Bangkok**

The owner of this English pub first installed a Western-style toilet and urinal to cater to the tourist trade. The resident clientele, however, persisted in using the toilet the local way, climbing up on to the toilet seat and squatting. Many broken toilet seats and thousands of Thai baht later, the proprietor had a classic Thai squat installed as well. Breakage was reduced, as patrons had the choice of a Western or a Thai toilet. As a result, the only facility in this pub is a cramped but eclectic mix of toilets.

223

**Gold Market Complex
Khajuraho
Madhya Pradesh**

And behind door number six is … a Western toilet! The stall doors of this public toilet, mysteriously, are numbered. Stalls one through five are typical squat toilets. They are flushed by filling a jug of water from a tap on the wall and dumping it down the toilet. The taps are not always properly turned off, which explains why this is the wettest part of town.

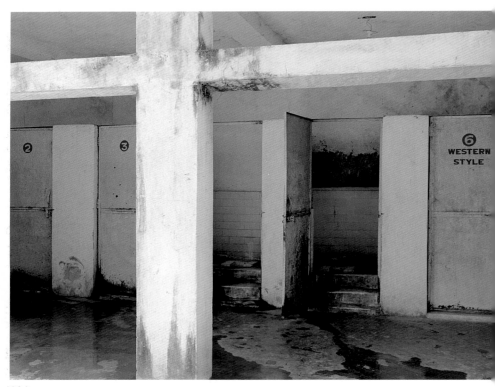

**Sulabh International
Museum of Toilets
Mahavir Enclave
Palam Dabri Road
New Delhi**

'Close stools' were common among the wealthy in Europe from the Middle Ages until the nineteenth century. A step up from squatting over a chamber pot, the close stool allowed the user to sit comfortably. Under a locking hinged lid, there was a seat with a removable bucket or chamber pot beneath. Later models were incorporated into furniture, such as this leather armchair close stool. They were gradually replaced by outhouses, owing largely to the Victorian disgust with bodily functions and the desire to conceal them whenever possible.

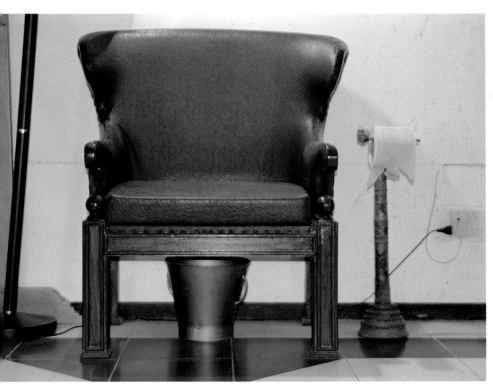

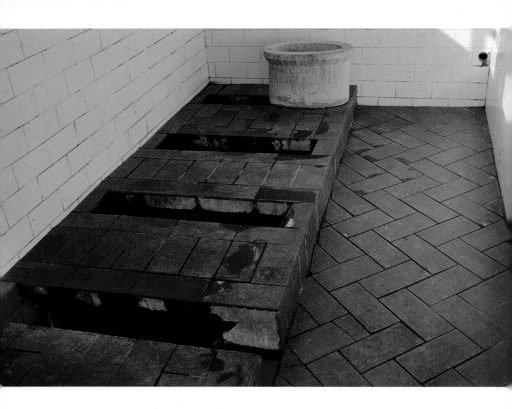

**Hutong
Beijing**

In the face of post-Communist modernization, Beijing's hutongs are the living remnants of the city's historical lifestyle. Unique to Chinese culture, hutongs are made up of quadrangles that were built as extensions to the Imperial city. Today these old enclosed neighbourhoods are made up of low houses and shops that line a warren of narrow lanes. Public toilets are common and are used by the families of the hutong and passers-by alike. The three holes and unusual facility for sitting have a trough below with running water to whisk waste away.

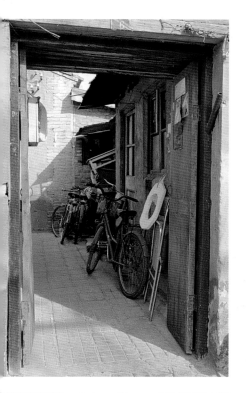

Families living near the common toilets have no need of their own. This family unhooks its own Styrofoam toilet seat, takes it to the public facilities and places it on the concrete receptacle shown opposite.

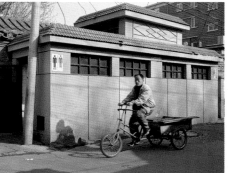

Outside view of the public toilets.

China

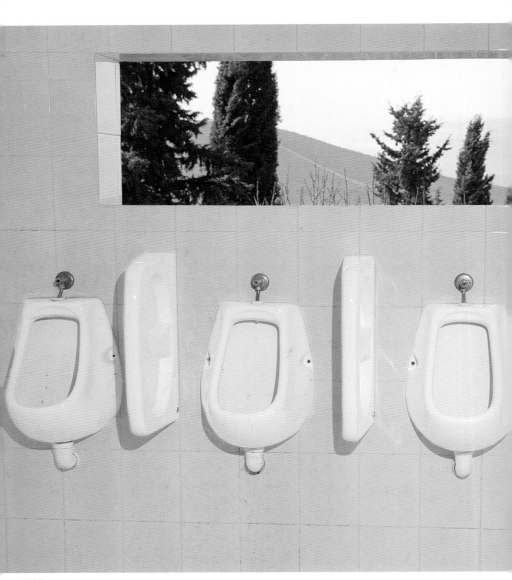

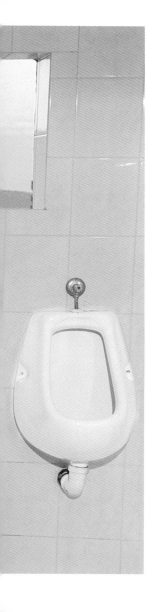

House of the Virgin Mary
Bülbül Mountain
Selçuk

While using these urinals, pilgrims can gaze out over the sublime panorama allegedly beheld by the Virgin Mary from AD 37 to 45. It is here that John the Baptist is said to have brought her from Jerusalem after the crucifixion of her son, Jesus Christ, and where she is supposed to have lived until her death at the age of sixty-four. The site of the Virgin Mary's house draws Christian pilgrims from all over the world.

**Katchpura
Agra
Uttar Pradesh**

In a valiant attempt to reduce the unsanitary practice of relief in random locations, public toilets have been installed in some rural Indian villages. This pinkish toilet building was made using the local clay. The women on the road are undoubtedly going to or from the toilet. The clue to their destination is the water bottle each holds. In lieu of toilet paper, the locals use water and their left hands.

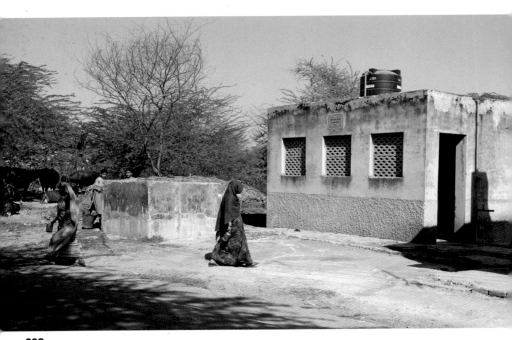

Garden Bowl Restaurant
54 Sha Mian Street
Shamian Island
Guangzhou

A few stairs must be mounted in order to reach this squat toilet, set in a colourful mosaic tile floor. Interestingly, this toilet is equipped with a short, miniature toilet tank. Shamian Island boasts a wealth of fine restaurants such as the Garden Bowl to satisfy its steady stream of foreign visitors. In the area one sees numerous Western couples with Chinese babies: tiny Shamian Island is the place where all the adoption administration of the world's most populated country is completed. The surplus of adoptable babies in China is due to the government's strictly enforced policy of one child per couple.

China

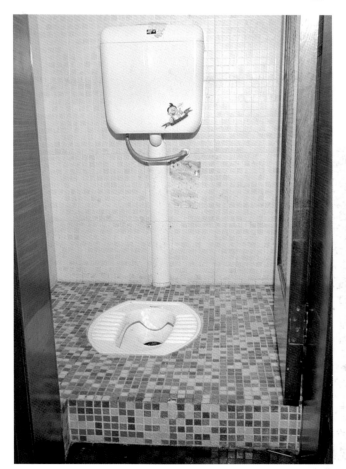

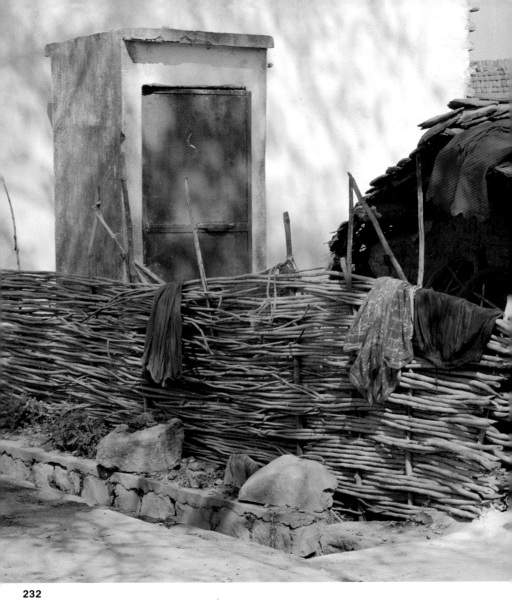

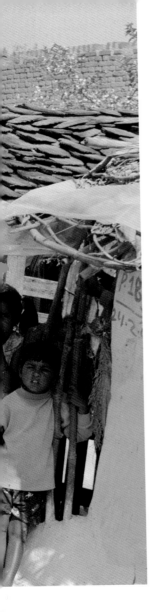

San Kargad
Khajuraho
Madhya Pradesh

To curb the unhealthy conditions provoked by open defecation, the Indian government initiated a programme to provide family toilets in rural villages. The inhabitants of this village relieved themselves in the nearby lake, then drank, bathed and washed clothing and cooking utensils in the same water. When each family received its government-issue outhouse, they were delighted with their new storage shed. Most continue to use the lake as their communal bathroom. Indian health officials are coming to realize that there cannot be sanitation in the absence of education.

Shivsagar Lake: the site of choice for drinking, washing and defecating.

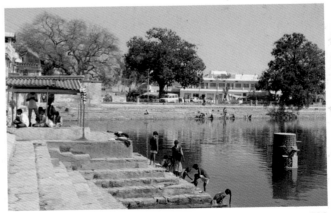

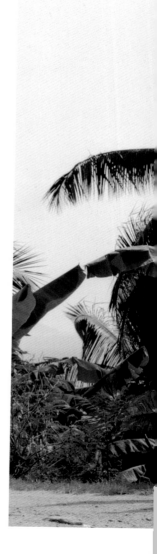

Thailand

Laem Bongson
Between Thong Sala
and Haadrin
Bantai
Koh Phangan

Partially hidden by banana
and papaya trees, this
outhouse sits on a hillside
overlooking the South China
Sea. It is a squat facility for
the nearby open-air roadside
bar. A pipe about 15 metres
(50 ft) long extends from
the back of the toilet. The
contents are expelled
through the pipe and burst
out into mid-air halfway
down the side of the cliff.
Fortunately, the end of
the pipe is out of sight and
the beach below inaccessible
for swimming.

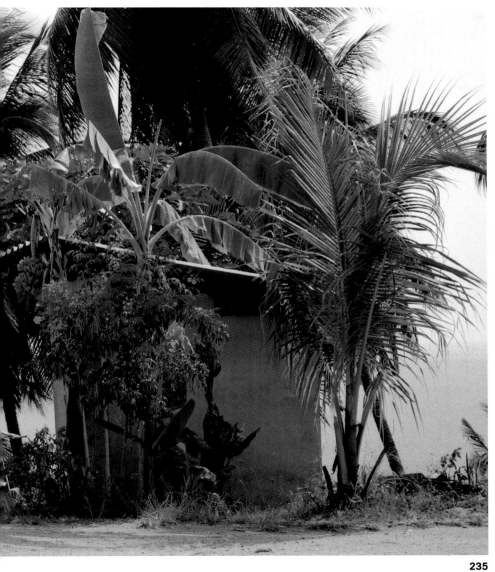

Asmalıbağ Şarap Evi
Şirince
İzmir

The squat is the most common type of toilet in Turkey. In fact, the French refer to all squats generically as *toilettes turques*, or Turkish toilets. Toilet paper is hardly used in this part of the world, where water is preferred. In this case, the user fills the jug from the tap beside the toilet and proceeds to clean himself with water and the left hand. This method is widely practised throughout the country, where the use of toilet paper is considered dirty.

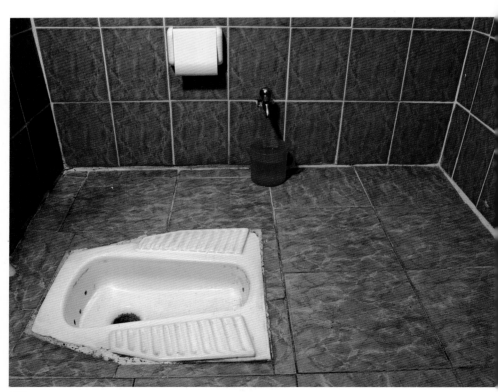

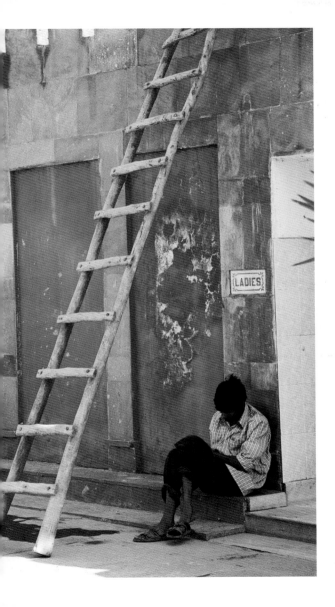

LADIES

Agra Fort
Agra
Uttar Pradesh

The formidable red sandstone Agra Fort doubled as a palace and a military stronghold. It was rebuilt by the great Mughal emperor Akbar in 1565. His grandson, Shah Jahan, built the neighbouring jewel that is the Taj Mahal. Even the modern visitors' toilets at Agra Fort are made of the striking red sandstone. In the heat of the afternoon, the non-superstitious toilet attendant breaks for a nap under his ladder.

237

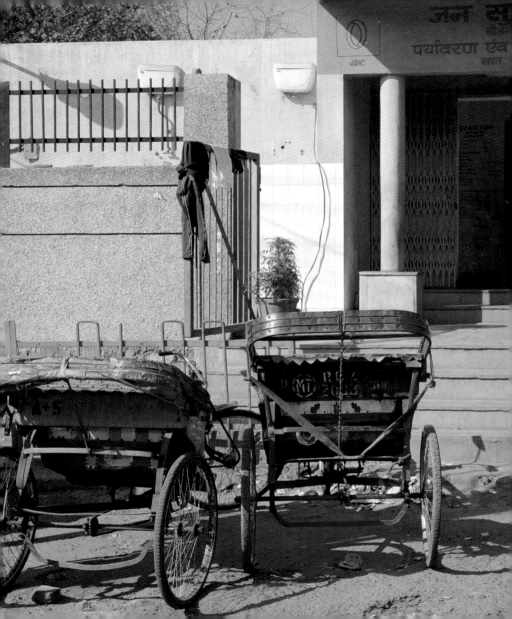

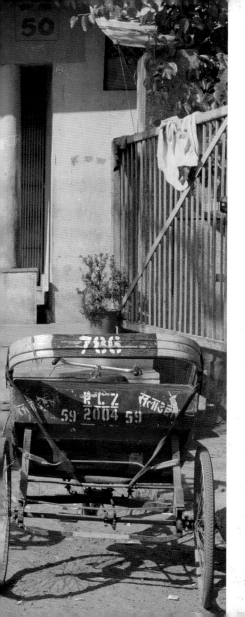

**Matya Mahal
Shahjahanabad (Old Delhi)
Delhi**

Three rickshaw drivers make a pit stop at this public toilet, one of thousands constructed and maintained by the Sulabh Sanitation Movement in India. With visionary perseverance, Sulabh leads the quest for improved sanitary conditions in the country. By promoting the use of well-maintained flush toilets, the spread of disease is reduced. Of equal, if not greater, importance are the humanitarian implications of the improved facilities: the abolition of the need for scavengers. The lowest of all Indian castes, the 'untouchables', representing generations of scavengers, inherit the subhuman profession of emptying and removing waste from non-flush toilets.

239

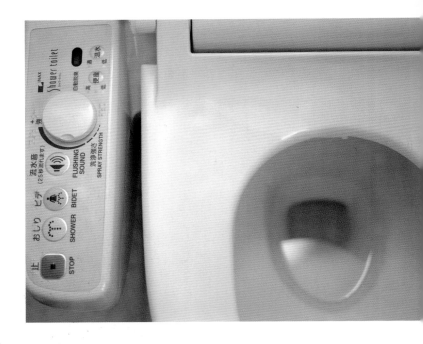

Shiodome Siosite
Ginza
Tokyo

'Sweet treat' is the first term that comes to mind to describe this toilet. The whole blissful experience begins with the seat, heated to a delicious temperature. Before getting down to business, the sound button comes to the rescue of those shy in public places: a loud canned flushing noise may be played at will to fool the neighbouring cubicles. Assuming that more than flushing has taken place, the remaining buttons may be put to use: 'bidet' for a soothing spray of water on the general posterior area, 'shower' for a strategically aligned hard, straight jet. Water temperature and spray strength may be adjusted before moving on to the blow-dry cycle, finishing up with a jet of warm or cool air. The next visit is eagerly anticipated.

hsinağa Mosque
tatürk Mahallesi
nd Kizilay Caddesi
elçuk

efore entering to pray in a
iosque, the faithful remove
ieir footwear and wash
ecause shoes are strictly
orbidden in the house of
llah. Wash stations are
ound just outside the
mosque and sometimes
double as the local public
toilet. The entrance to these
underground toilets can be
seen on the left, where there
is a booth to pay the fee for a
pee. The call to prayer blares
loudly from the minarets of
each mosque, beckoning
everyone to pray (and
therefore wash) five times
each day.

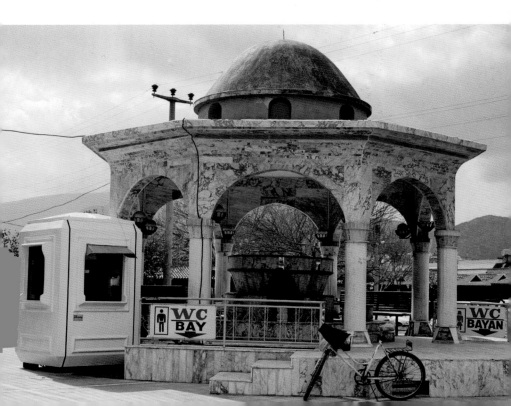

**Lumphini Park
Rama IV Road
Bangkok**

This unusually shaped toilet is a common version of the Thai squat. The user steps up and places a foot on each footpad, facing forward. The only way to flush a squat in Siam is to dump a bucket of water down it. The water trough and bowl serve this purpose. Paper goes in the bin and not the toilet, as the plumbing in much of Thailand is delicate and paper will quickly clog the pipes.

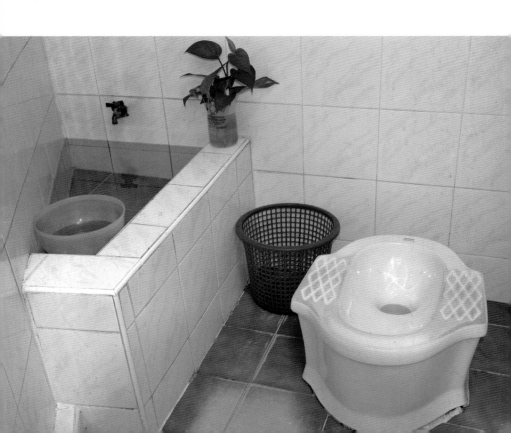

Felix Restaurant
The Peninsula Hong Kong
Salisbury Road
Kowloon

Situated on the twenty-eighth floor of the Peninsula Hotel, these elegant black column urinals enhance an otherwise mundane experience. A miniature waterfall activated by an electric eye starts to flow down the back of the urinal when the user approaches. As if standing at a podium, the client can gaze out over the expanse of neon lights that is the sprawling city of Kowloon. Felix's posh restaurant, bar and urinals were designed by Philippe Starck.

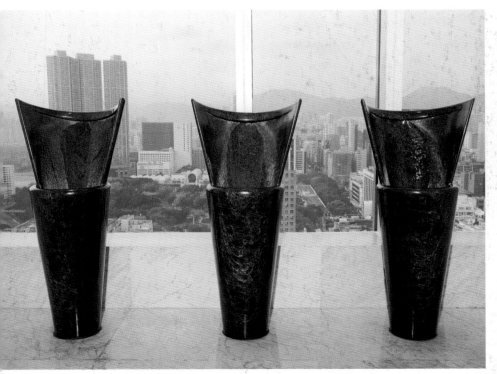

Damola
City of Panna
Madhya Pradesh

In India it is common for houses to have outdoor toilets. This three-hole family toilet once offered more privacy, but all that remains now is the door frame. The house is built above street level, so whatever goes into the toilet slides down to the narrow alleyway below. This type of toilet does not need cleaning, as the local feral pigs come by regularly. Just able to fit in the alley, each morning the toilet cleaners gleefully feast on the delectable morsels offered in the night.

A cow – held sacred by Hindus – and a feral pig feed on garbage.

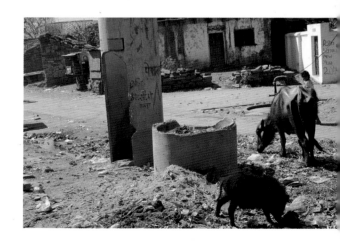

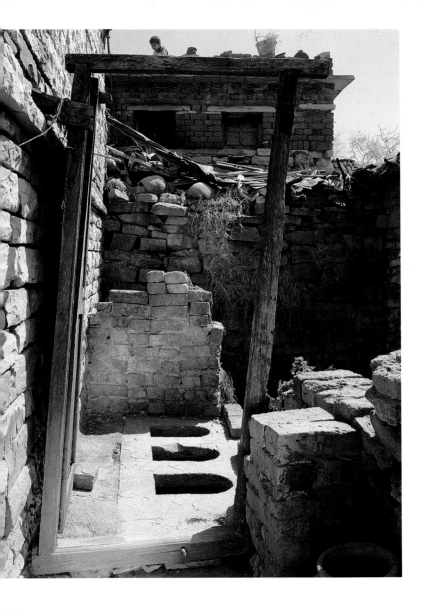

**Great Wall of China
Simatai entrance
Border between Hebei and
Beijing Shi provinces**

Pilgrims to the Great Wall of
China are strongly urged to
use these facilities before
trekking up the wall, as there
is none along its 6700 km
(4200 mile) length. From the
keyhole-shaped entrance to
these surprisingly modern
toilets, visitors get their
first glimpse of one of
the greatest human
accomplishments on earth.
Construction of the Great
Wall began in the third
century and it was expanded
and rebuilt by successive
dynasties through to the
fifteenth century. Although
it proved to be a formidable
barrier, it failed in its ultimate
purpose of protecting the
Chinese throne from a
succession of marauders from
the north. Most notably, in
the thirteenth century the
notorious Genghis Khan
simply bribed the sentries to
let him cross the wall with his
bloodthirsty Mongolian army.

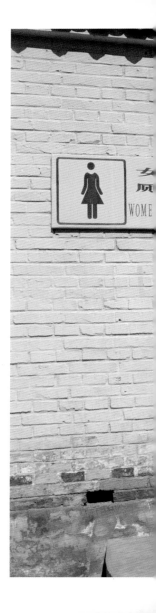

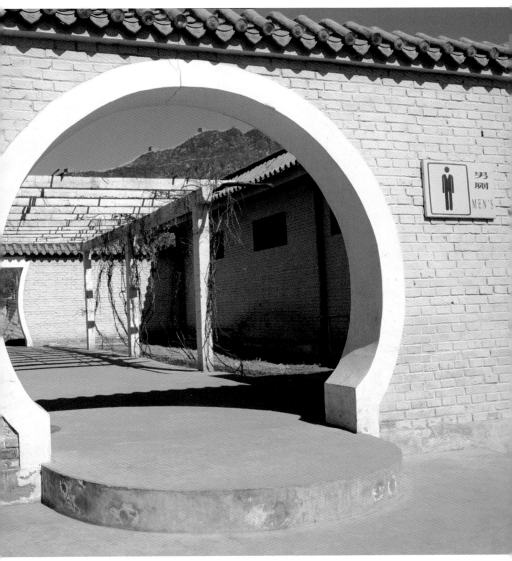

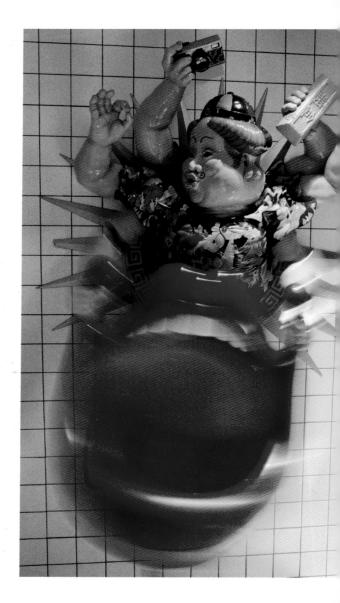

Ten & Chi
Lemina Building
Shinjuku
Tokyo

If there were awards for the
most entertaining toilets,
this Tokyo restaurant would
take the gold. When the
unsuspecting client steps
up to the urinal (yes, it is a
urinal), the unit suddenly
roars to life. Music blares and
the huge laughing mouth
swings from side to side.
The user must also sway with
the music to avoid soiling the
floor. The head above the
urinal spins round and round,
cackling. This life-sized
mutant takes pictures, flash
and all, holding its camera in
one of six hands.

248

Like an effective movie, this ensemble of toilets entertains, evokes high emotion and plays on fear and insecurity. The imposing man-toilet is a fine specimen of this freakish collection. Each of the urinals suspended from his yoke moves up and down. The giant suddenly utters a long, satisfied moan. Then in a booming voice, he compliments the belittled user on the appearance of his member. "That's a nice one you have!" is the rough translation from Japanese. Meanwhile, his own monstrous endowment is bursting from his tight shorts. He then reprimands the unsettled user, telling him he's standing too far back and is splashing the floor. Throughout the ordeal, the giant leers at the patron with wanton perversion.

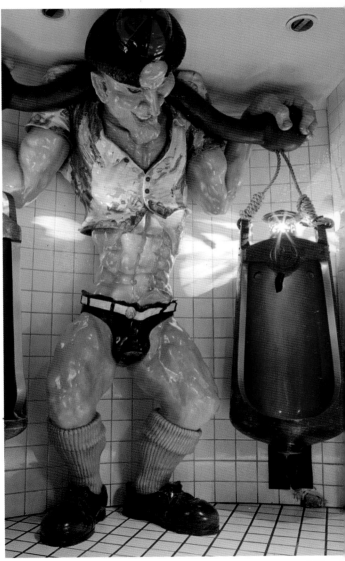

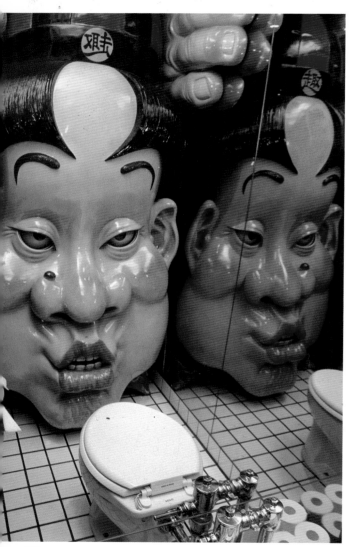

This is arguably the most moving toilet experience a woman can have. Once the user is comfortably seated, the gargantuan floor-to-ceiling head slowly starts advancing. Loud, frenzied music with maniacal singing begins to blare. This part is terrifying – the woman's heart races as she envisions herself being crushed to bits by the monstrous head. The looming head finally stops just in front of her, planting a larger-than-life kiss on her knees.

another of these absolutely urreal toilets, the lady sits own in this seemingly nremarkable toilet stall. She aces a pair of ornate double oors the size of the pposing wall. When she's early done, she reaches for he toilet paper. The cubicle uddenly goes pitch black and he massive doors slowly ving open, groaning loudly. erie light emanates from ithin, illuminating a ghastly, eated figure. Cackling shrilly bove the rumble of thunder, he androgynous freak slowly reeps out, reaching towards he frightened woman. uspended from two gnarly ngers is a roll of toilet paper. nce the lady has made use f this offering, the freak ecedes back into its lair, the oors creak shut and the ghting returns to normal.

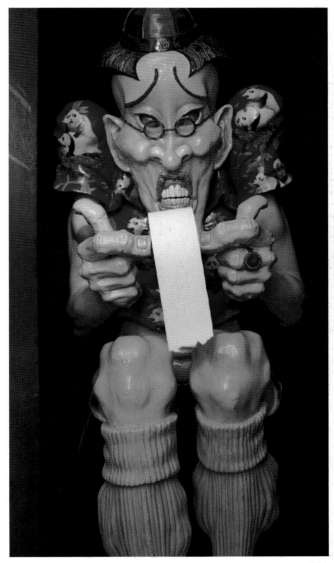

Books

D. Abram *et al.*, *The Rough Guide to India,* 5th edn,
London (Rough Guides) 2003

M. Blair, *Bathroom Ceramics,*
Princes Risborough, UK (Shire Publications) 2003

S. Doggett, *Panama,* 2nd edn,
Footscray, Australia (Lonely Planet Publications) 2001

J.L. Horan, *The Porcelain God: A Social History of the Toilet,*
Secaucus NJ (Carol Publishing Group) 1997

R. Kilroy, *The Compleat Loo: A Lavatorial Miscellany,*
London and New York (Victor Gollancz/
Barnes & Noble Books) 1984

L. Lambton, *Temples of Convenience and Chambers of Delight,*
London (Pavilion Books) 1995

D. Leffman *et al.*, *The Rough Guide to China,* 3rd edn,
London (Rough Guides) 2003

B. Pathak, *Road to Freedom: A Sociological Study on the
Abolition of Scavenging in India,*
Delhi (Motilal Banarsidass Publishers Private Limited) 1991

S.P. Singh, *Sulabh Sanitation Movement,* 3rd edn,
New Delhi (Sulabh International Social Service
Organization) 2002

Reference Websites

Musings of a Privy Digger: www.bottlebooks.com/privyto.htm
City Population: www.citypopulation.de
The Lost Gardens of Heligan, Cornwall:
www.cornwall-calling.co.uk/homes-and-gardens/ heligan.htm
*H. Holmes (1997) The Skinny On ... Why Toilet Bowl Water
Twirls Clockwise:*
www.discovery.com/area/skinnyon/skinnyon970523/
skinny1.html
Most Expensive Washroom:
www.guinnessworldrecords.com/index.asp?ID=56573
The Bridge on the River Kwai:
www.history.acusd.edu/gen/filmnotes/bridgekwai.html
History of Toilets:
www.interiordesign.net/index.asp?
layout=id_green&articleid=CA512462
Outhouses of America Tour: www.jldr.com/index.html
Toilets: www.menstuff.org/issues/byissue/toilets.html

Water Use – Facts and Figures:
  www.ollierecycles.com/planet/usa/info/info/wause15.htm
The History of Plumbing in Crete:
  www.plumbingsupply.com/pmcrete.html
History of Plumbing – Roman and English Legacy:
  www.plumbingsupply.com/pmroman.html
Thomas Crapper: Myth & Reality:
  www.plumbingsupply.com/pmthomas.html
The Men That Made the Water Closet:
  www.plumbingsupply.com/pmtoilet.html
The Amish:
  www.religiousmovements.lib.virginia.edu/nrms/amish.html
Pablo Escobar Gaviria:
  www.rotten.com/library/bio/crime/criminals/pablo-escobar/
Flushed with Pride:
  www.stoke.gov.uk/museums/gladstone/gpmflushed.htm
History of Plumbing: www.theplumber.com /#history
Australia's National Public Toilet Map: www.toiletmap.gov.au

Toilet Websites
CWS BestCleanSeat:
  www.cws.com/servlet/PB/menu/1020577/index.html
Falcon Waterfree Urinals: www.falconwaterfree.com/ flash.htm
Thomas Crapper History:
  www.thomas-crapper.com/history02.asp
Villeroy & Boch Oblic:
  www.villeroy-boch.com/Oblic.93.0.html?&C=CA&L=en
www.cromwell-intl.com/toilet
www.philippe-starck.com
www.thebathroomdiaries.com
www.toiletmuseum.com
www.toiletnet.com
www.urinal.net
www.worldtoilet.info

Acknowledgements

We would like to express our gratitude to all the people and establishments who allowed us to photograph this multitude of interesting and unusual toilets. Thanks to our toilet guides and to everyone who contributed toilet locations, told us their toilet tales (everyone has one) or otherwise helped us out along the way. We apologize that we don't have all your names (often we couldn't even speak your language), but without you this book would be very different. We sincerely appreciate it.

In North America:
Dr Don Rethke (aka Dr Flush) and the New England Air Museum; Jean McHarg; Bob and Mary Fulleman; the crew of USS *Pampanito*; the crew of USS *Hornet*; Lorena and Dave Lonergan; Tanya Godard; Ronald Maillet; Christoph Roher; Andrew Wienser; the bartender of the Whiskey Café; Christopher A. Rudolf.

In Central and South America:
Juan of Arequipa; Edwin of Cuzco; Luis of Drake's Bay; Stephen Hodges from Kentucky; Martin Skoda (the brave snorkeller).

In Europe:
Angela Lee of the Gladstone Pottery Museum; the North Stafford Hotel; Paul Brown and Mo Kok; Richard Strong; Helena Koot; Philippe Candael; Xavier and Daphne of restaurant Aux Enfants Terribles.

In Africa:
Sérgio Mahumane; Ruard Ganzevoort; Inspector Charles; Evan and Corlia Roberts of Diamond Diggers Lodge; Crazy Dave at the Old Vic Travellers Inn; Henny Pretorius; Benjy Francis; Arthur Long; Amir and Liat of Tel Aviv; the guys at Underdog Productions, Jo'burg, RSA.

In Oceania:
Dean Rathgen; Jenny Rathgen; the Geraldine cocky and his thousands of sheep; staff and friends of the Victoria Hotel and Pub in Ouyen; Denis O'Leary and his dog.

In Asia:
Mehmet Nazli; Iqbal Khan; Laloo Biscarma; Dr Bindeshwar Pathek and Bageshwar Jha of Sulabh International Museum of Toilets; Mikio Ogasawara and staff of Ten and Chi Restaurant.